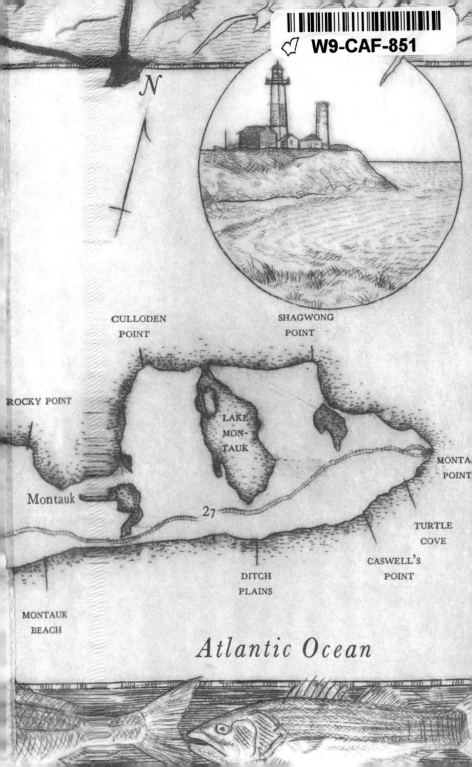

N

CULLODEN
POINT

SHAGWONG
POINT

ROCKY POINT

LAKE
MON-
TAUK

MONTA
POINT

Montauk

27

TURTLE
COVE

CASWELL'S
POINT

DITCH
PLAINS

MONTAUK
BEACH

*Atlantic Ocean*

# THE MOON PULLED UP AN ACRE OF BASS

# THE MOON PULLED UP AN ACRE OF BASS

A Flyrodder's Odyssey
at Montauk Point

## PETER KAMINSKY

AN IMPRINT OF HYPERION
NEW YORK

Library of Congress Cataloging-in-Publication Data

Kaminsky, Peter.
    The moon pulled up an acre of bass : a flyrodder's odyssey at Montauk Point /
Peter Kaminsky.—1st ed.
        p. cm.
    ISBN: 0-7868-6769-8
    1. Saltwater fly fishing—New York—Montauk Point.    2. Fishes—Migration—
New York—Montauk Point.    3. Montauk Point (N.Y.)    I. Title.

SH529.K35 2001
799.1'24'0974725—dc21                                                    2001024468

*Book design by Casey Hampton*

FIRST EDITION

10 9 8 7 6 5 4 3 2 1

for Melinda

# Acknowledgments

≋

My thanks to Susan Adams, Jay Cassel, Duncan Barnes and Bill Breen for giving me the assignments that made it okay with the family to fish the East End. To hundreds of anglers from whom I have learned over the years, in particular, Gene Calgero on the Esopus Creek and Jack Allen in the Everglades. On the East End: John Groth, Jim Clark, Sam Lester, Harvey Bennett, Jim Levison, David Blinken, Ernie French, Tim O'Rourke, Wally Johnsen and, most of all, Amanda Switzer and Paul Dixon. Kathy Hattala and Vic Vecchio of the Department of Environmental Conservation for sharing their deep knowledge of the striped bass. Also Heidi O'Riordan and Polly Weigand. The last haul seine crew, Jens and Mitchell Lester, Walter and Wally Bennett and Mickey Miller. Russell Drumm of *The East Hampton Star* for his generosity with contacts and knowledge collected over a lifetime of writing about the East End. Bill Akin for his priceless tapes. Betty Franey for her house and its stove. Bryan Miller for his friendship (and introducing me to Betty). Jacques and Trish Franey for keeping my glass full. Kurt Andersen for advising me to write about pleasure and Mark Reiter my friend and agent, who kept bugging me to actually do it. Also at IMG,

Carolyn Krupp, Anne Torrago, Maris Kreizman and Michelle Yung. Glenn Wolff for the drawings that gave life to many of my *New York Times* columns over the years (as well as the endpapers of this book). My editor, Gretchen Young, for her boundless reserves of encouragement and smarts. Her associate, Natalie Kaire, for keeping things pleasantly on track. Tom Akstens, Scott Bowen, Guy Martin and Melinda for reading so carefully and responding so thoughtfully. Tracey Winningham for listening and making sense of it all. Vivian Holtzman and Jason Biondo for tracking down answers. Nick Lyons and John Waller Hills for their flyfishing books about a time and place. Gray Kunz for his friendship and cuisine, in that order. Alain Ducasse for his steak recipe. My mom and her mom for their brisket recipe. My dad and his dad for their love of writing. Andrea and Sharon at The Springs General Store for being open early and late. And, finally, until someone proves otherwise, thanks to Johnny Appleseed, who I am sure planted the wonderful Macoun apples that are at their crispest and sweetest when the stripers are running.

*Sometimes dreams, even those of a fisherman, come true.*

—ZANE GREY, *Tales of Fishing Virgin Seas*

Part One

READY FOR THE RUN

# Accabonac Neck

≋

THE AIR SMELLS SALTY and grassy and flowery all at once. I walk through a stand of daisies onto the sea wall in front of my house. *Must be fish happening. It looks so right.*

I phone Paul Dixon. He is on his boat, guiding flyfishermen somewhere between Montauk Point and Gardiners Island in front of me.

"Where are you?" he asks.

"On Gerard Drive. Fifth house from the end."

"Then you should see me, I'm at Accabonac Neck. The albacore have been feeding on the falling tide all afternoon."

"I don't see you, Paul, I see a boat by the green buoy."

"Then you must see me."

I don't. I'm stumped. I clearly marked my house in relation to Accabonac Neck when I fished here a month ago. Of course, I was concentrating on fish then more than houses. Apparently, I had been nowhere near the fifth house. Chalk my misdirection up to the same mental mechanism that causes anglers to mis-remember the size of fish. It has nothing to do with lying. It has everything to do with good fishing making you a little light headed—somewhere between rapture and a moderate wine buzz.

I drive down to the Neck. Paul's boat is gone by then, but in the slackening tide rip I see false albacore feeding. Not what you would call a blitz—the term that locals use to describe a frenzy of game fish close to shore. Still, there is enough happening to excite me. The albacore—a warm water fish whose arrival in Indian summer is the overture to the fishing of the fall—cut foamy white slashes in the surface as they porpoise through the schools of baitfish. Coy, but catchable.

My heart pounds. Unbidden, a tune takes over in my head, a typical event in my angling mindscape. Though I love practically everything about fishing, the way you start humming a tune at the beginning of a fishing session that becomes your mantra until you finish fishing can be vexsome if your internal jukebox has bad taste. However, on this, the first day of my angling odyssey, Johnny Mercer's "Don't Mess With Mr. In Between" kicks in. I can deal with that.

I walk up to a man with a volunteer fire department emblem on his shirt. He watches the fish working.

"Anything doing?" I ask.

"Albacore. They've been here for hours."

We watch a ten-year-old boy fight and land an albacore, bright green and blue and silver.

I speed home and throw my canoe on top of the car. I fumble with the canoe tie-down straps. I know that if I wait to rig my flyrod until I return to the Neck where all those feeding fish are in plain view, I will screw up. So I perform the whole operation in the driveway. I take my old Orvis rod—a twelve-year-old graphite that I am told is an artless warclub but which has served me well—and string it up with flyline of the same vintage. The leader looks good enough, I hope. I tie on a small epoxy fly, an imitation of the bay anchovy on which the albies are feeding. These anchovies are also called rainbait, because on a calm sea they dimple the surface like rain. They sound like rain too: a soft steady rain on a wooden roof.

Back at the Neck, I carry my lightweight canoe and paddle in one hand, my rod in the other. In my urgency I have forgotten my water shoes at the house, so I walk barefoot, as if on nails, over the gravel at the water's edge. I sit in the canoe and push off.

The light breeze nudges me toward the albacore. In a canoe, even more so than in a motor-powered craft, you pray for the albies to stay in one place. Like a classroom full of rambunctious first-graders they never stop moving. You must try mightily not to disturb them or they will bolt and you will be chasing, but not catching, fish all afternoon.

If you can ease yourself into position, you may get a shot. Then, if you cast fast and true, you will hook up. If you choose the right fly and you do not hook a fish, it means you didn't get the fly in front of the fish. Cast well and you will succeed.

Easy to say.

I stroke with my double-sided paddle. The canoe tracks beautifully. I move among the fish with barely a wake. I strip off thirty feet of line from the reel. The wind pushes my stern around making it difficult to keep the canoe stable while firing off a cast. The image comes to mind of a ranch hand trying to lasso a calf in a corral of circling steers.

The fish move off. I follow. We head away from the Neck toward my house. I am now a third of the way across the strait to Gardiners Island, a mile in the distance. The afternoon sun reflects off the light chop on the water, lighting it up like fluttering birch leaves turned autumn yellow.

Two monarch butterflies pass within a few feet of me. At the beginning of the autumn run there are always monarch butterflies dancing above the waves. Riding the breeze like tufts of orange and black gift wrapping, they look impossibly fragile against the backdrop of tropical storms, rushing tides and heaving seas. At night, when they roost in the trees, resting on their flight south to Mexico, they look like Christmas ornaments on the branches of the evergreens. The pair in front of me take their time. I watch them for a long while.

Herman Melville, at the very beginning of *Moby Dick*, says, "As everyone knows, meditation and water are wedded forever." At moments like these, when the world looks like a rose window in a cathedral; when your mind, like my canoe, simply drifts; when you don't know if it is five minutes or fifty minutes that go by before you wake from your daydream, I fully understand his meaning.

The fish ball up again, herding the bait. The birds hover then dive into the compacted school. I stroke twice, lay down the paddle and cast. An albacore hits my fly. I attempt to strike back, but my presentation is off. You must cast in a straight line with no slack in it and strike hard to set the hook as soon as the albie hits. If the cast is off or half a second late, the odds are against you from the start.

The school stays around. This time I connect. I watch the albacore turn its side to me as it gulps the fly. Then an alarming thought: *What do I do if this fish tows me all around the bay?* There really is no way to stop it and the albacore is a blistering runner.

Furthermore, if I am going to try to tire it by moving the tip of the rod to and fro, I will need to execute that maneuver forcefully but delicately. Otherwise I will swamp my canoe.

The fish tears off for deep water. I let it bend the rod way more than they say is good for it. For the first time in a long time, I hope for a small fish. I am not in practice to fight and land a big one. My hopes are answered as a small albacore surrenders. I grab it around the tail, lay my rod down and unhook it. It shoots off like a ray of light.

First day, first fish. Hopefully, a portent of good things to come, but I know from experience that a good day in September means little. Bluefish must come to stay to provide brutish power to the angling mix. And striped bass must appear daily at the Point to truly satisfy the flyfishing connoisseur. The bass, who were so wary in the summer, throw caution to the winds and gather each autumn in a Dionysian riot. Although a great autumn will always start with the albacore coming, as they did today, into the bay to feed in the warm shallows, a lot of other things have to go right for a memorable season to follow.

# Serengeti By-the-Sea

≋

RIGHT AFTER LABOR DAY, as the summer folk depart, a thousand mile-convoy of striped bass, bluefish, weakfish, shad, tuna, albacore, anchovies, menhaden, blueback herring, sharks, whales, and dolphins begins to pass by Montauk Point on the way south.

This yearly march past the end of Long Island is among the largest wildlife migrations on earth. I believe it is, in fact, the biggest migration anywhere on our planet. I have posed this to a number of scientists—oceanographers, marine biologists, ecologists—and at first they look doubtful. Then I explain my theory and I usually get, "I don't think anybody has thought of it in quite that way before. You may well be right."

It starts with the simple observation that there is a lot of life on the move. There are millions of bass, tuna, bluefish, sea mammals, waterfowl, song birds, and monarch butterflies coursing down our coast. Then factor in the bait schools: billions of creatures in the clouds of smaller fry that color the waves. In pure numbers of individuals, it dwarfs any migration on land.

Add in the fact that the watery prairies that extend from the

Grand Banks off Newfoundland and the Georges Banks off Massachusetts are among the most fecund waters on the planet. There are other places as productive of life—off Antarctica, and between Japan and Kamchatka—but the combination of cold waters that teem with life in the shorter summers at high latitudes and a thousand miles of estuaries likewise filled with warmer water creatures, is unique to the Atlantic seaboard. Most of the northerly fish that live on the Banks, and in the coastal shallows move south come fall. All of them funnel into the water between the coast and the gulf stream. The neck of that funnel, its narrowest part, is where the Montauk headland meets the ocean. From the lighthouse to the gulf stream, a tide of life.

Think of the fishing at Montauk, or any place where migrating creatures and the environment interact, as a large orchestra that gets together for a few weeks every year. For good music to be made, the instruments must be in tune. Are they fairly balanced—are there just enough trumpets to soar over the violins? Can the conductor balance all those competing egos (and control his own)?

The variables that affect the migration and therefore the angling at Montauk, part physical, part biological, are similarly interrelated. There is the well-known effect of the jet stream, pulling down cold air from the north and pushing up warmth from the south. Then there is the gulf stream. Similar to the factors that create El Niño in the Pacific, there are similar oscillations of atmospheric pressure in the Atlantic that steer the gulf stream some years closer to land, others further offshore. As early as the seventeenth century the inhabitants of Greenland noticed the effects of these oscillations. When their winter was cold, Denmark's was mild and vice versa. It is only recently that scientists have learned that this pattern is a function of whether the gulf stream moves north or south according to the air pressure differences in the Atlantic.

If the pressure is low off Iceland, the north wall of the stream drifts away from the equator and allows warm air masses to move north from the tropics while keeping cold water from flowing down the continental shelf off the Atlantic coast. In this case, if there has been a lot of summertime heat off the coast of Africa, you may reasonably count on tropical storms to bear down on New England. If, on the other hand, the gulf stream has moved south and the tropics are calm, the door will open for northeasters and northwesters to bring unrelieved cold winds and currents that will drive the bait offshore. Where the bait goes, the gamefish follow. Which of these factors starts the cascade of events that leads to the fishing conditions outside my door on Gardiners Bay is something science has yet to determine. The fact remains, though, that this metaphorical orchestra has a lot of instruments that need to be in tune for me to have happy angling.

Last year was an out of tune year. For the first time that I can remember, there were no fish on the beaches or at the Point. Two early season hurricanes with strong northeasters in between sent the bait offshore. The migration passed wide of Montauk. The fish never came back that year once their forage had been dispersed from Montauk.

The Law of Averages, that Nicene Creed of gamblers which causes them to double down on the next hand of blackjack, the next roll of the dice, convinced me that this year would be different because in Montauk, most years are great.

The key is bait. The confluence of currents, the narrowness of the passage at Montauk, and the temperature of the water causes bait to pause at the Point in October. When this happens, migrating predators likewise congregate. Spend a day here when Nature convenes her creatures. Big fish eating little fish. Everything fleeing south. Northeast gales pushing out September's warm waters. Life on the move.

I have sat in a blind in Africa waiting for the animals to come in to a water hole. There is something voyeuristic about watching a natural act in the wild. We modern humans are not far removed from our hunting ancestors, who for millions of years depended on game for their sustenance. I respond to the sight of wildlife, we all respond. You may not fish, you may not hunt, but your soul is that of a hunter, a fisher. It is in your genes. The sight of game will always move you. This connection, person-to-nature can be so intense that it will stay with you more fully than days, even months, of normal day-to-day existence.

I am sure that a similar passage of game across the tundras of Ice Age France inspired some Stone Age artist to descend into a limestone cave and draw his pictures of bison and mammoths on hidden cavern walls: beautiful spirits of the Hunted. For most of humanity's stay on the planet we have waited hungrily for migrations. The sight of masses of life on the move cannot help but quicken the blood and drive every other thought away. We are made that way. Find food, make babies, make art, that's what humans do.

We also flyfish.

If you love flyfishing as I do, as my friends at the Point do, you will, at times, forsake career and family, sobriety, sleep, food, and warmth for the chance to be on the water when the migration occurs. Every species is after something. My species, the flyfishing species, is after *morone saxatalis*, striped bass. After that, throw in albacore, bluefish, weakfish, and the occasional tuna.

Blessed by the geography that squeezes all the migrating animals into the neck of the oceanic funnel at Montauk, the Point also has an undersea geology particularly attractive to gamefish. Between the Point and Block Island the sea is a series of rips that give birth to currents that trap bait and render them vulnerable to predators such as the striper. These rips are formed when the tide moves over humps and depressions in the ocean floor. On a hump the tide is compressed and moves more swiftly. Over a depression, the moving water column is not as compressed and moves more leisurely.

Students of animals in the wild recognize this as a classic transition zone. Hunters and fishers think of it as the Edge, the place where prey are most susceptible. The Montauk seascape, from Shagwong Point on the northwest shore to Montauk Village on the south side, and extending from the headland at the lighthouse to Block Island, is blessed with hundreds of rips where the eternal contest between predator and prey plays out with great intensity each fall.

Ever since the delirious afternoon that I caught three dozen striped bass over 30 inches with Paul Dixon, I have wanted to flyfish the whole month of October from beginning to end. John Keats, in his ode "To Autumn," rhapsodizes it as a "Season of

mists and mellow fruitfulness,/Close bosom-friend of the ma-
turing sun." To be sure, ripening fields and languid Indian Summer days are part of what October is about, but at the Point,
October takes little notice of balmy afternoons and crisp apples.
In the currents and over the shoals, in the rocky coves and heaving seas, October is a crush of life—a living river that appears
to have no end. The yearly drama begins around the first of the
month, peaks near the middle, and usually moves to a third act
curtain by month's end.

Like most anglers, if I get to see it at all (some years I don't),
it is usually a day here, a day there. Always great, never enough.
In my daydreaming moments—I have many of them—I have
found myself wondering, *What would it be like to experience the
autumn run from its balmy start to its stormy finish?* But you know
how it goes. One deadline slams into another and all of a sudden
it's Christmas and the bass have retired to their winter quarters.

This year I made up my mind. "For the next month and a
half," I tell colleagues and friends, "what I am doing is fishing.
If you need to see me, come on out. And bring your rod."

### September 17

I throw my canoe on top of my Volvo, cram the car full of
fishing gear, fishing books, one Macintosh PowerBook, one
copy of Emily Dickinson, my Finnish fillet knife, two pairs of
jeans, a few T-shirts, two polar fleece pullovers and a rain jacket.
I pop a Lucinda Williams CD in the stereo and depart my home
in Brooklyn. Next stop, my home for the autumn at 107 Gerard
Drive, The Springs, East Hampton. A shallow strait of less than
a mile separates it from Gardiners Island, the largest piece of
undeveloped land on Long Island.

Behind my house, the mainland breaks the force of winds out of the west and northwest. Likewise, the bluffs on the sea-ward side of Gardiners Island temper the enthusiasm of all but the most powerful northeasters. On a clear day you can see past the island all the way to Montauk, some 21.6 miles east and slightly north. Across the bay and due south, the narrow isthmus known as Promised Land acts as a bulwark from the waves that pile up on the white sand beaches that face the Atlantic. If you wanted to order up a house with access to all the different kinds of fishable waters on the East End, you would be hard pressed to pick a better site than Gerard Drive.

It is even more of a find because this house comes with the most well equipped kitchen I have ever had. No million-dollar designer renovation here. There is a huge inferno of a stove—four blackened burners and a grill down the middle—knives for cutting every known edible, and pans galore. There is enough room to stack as many pots as I can dirty, enough counter space to rehearse a small marching band. You see, I have lucked into the kitchen of the late Pierre Franey, one of the greatest chefs in America from the 1950s through the early 1990s.

In 1996, Pierre was felled by a heart attack while serving as guest chef/instructor on a cruise ship. His wife, Betty, still sum-mers on Gerard Drive. She has agreed to let me have the place for the fall at what one can only regard as a philanthropic, friend-to-the-writer, rate.

A great house, a place to cook to my heart's content, and the whole month to fish every day. If the weather and the fish co-operate, I am positively bathing in blessings—champagne bottles of them.

# Bang!

≋

IN THE THIRD WEEK of September the sky is high and blue. The rolling clouds have a summery fluff to them. Gardiners Island, which looks close enough to touch on such days, is as pristine today as it was in the days when the Montaukett Indians camped here. Then as now, the tides washed through the inlet of Accabonac Harbor, about half a mile further down Gerard Drive from my house. Scallops, oysters and clams have always been bountiful in the sun-washed shallows. Baitfish, in particular bay anchovies which are favored in the autumn by bass, bluefish and albacore, are among the most numerous inhabitants.

The southwest wind that blows off the ocean on summer afternoons carries with it an all but invisible mist that softens the light so that everything has the glow of a Degas ballerina in the footlights. The painters call it Long Island light. It attracted Jackson Pollock to a home about a mile from the Franey place.

I settle in over the course of the next week, waiting for The Run, likewise, to set up at the Point. I eat sweet corn and fat beefsteak tomatoes dressed only with salt, pepper and olive oil. I buy them from Vicki, a friendly woman who operates the last farm stand between Amagansett and the Point. There is not an ounce of off-putting Hamptons fashionability about her well-stocked stand—just gnarly tomatoes (the kind that are full of flavor), crisp white cauliflower, spinach, chard, beans and freshly dug potatoes that have an earthy and creamy deliciousness. Vicki is friendly, the service is personal. That makes all the difference to me.

I make daily (make that twice daily) calls to my guide friends. They are running all over Gardiners Bay looking for bass. When the albies are in strong they fish them, but everyone, myself included, looks for bass. I canoe along the tidal flat on Gerard Drive, a favored striper haunt during the summer. I find bluefish and albacore but no striped bass. They have moved out of the bays and shallows following the bay anchovies. The hope is they will reconvene and hook up with their migrating siblings at the Point.

On September 22, Paul Dixon is out with a charter and reports: "The fishing came off at the Point, *big time!*"

If there is to be a run, then this event will mark its beginning. The next day, Amanda Switzer and Josh Feigenbaum—the East End's newest guide and my oldest fishing partner—meet me at Rick's Crabby Cowboy on Lake Montauk. It is a family friendly honkytonk where Dixon moors his boats.

We putt-putt out of Montauk Harbor in a Hewes Light Tackle, a shallow draft skiff designed for moving along the tidal flats with a push pole and sneaking up noiselessly on fish. This is what the summer fishing is all about. In the autumn swells that often roll in on Montauk, the skiff is less than ideal and it occasionally provides a heart-stopping ride. But on this day the sea is calm and the air sweet. The sleepy summer port shows signs of energizing for the fall. Commercial fishermen in boats large and small make their way out of the harbor. Amanda, a good-looking athletic woman with long, sandy blond hair, waves to a friend who tows his rusty but reliable old trawler over to the boatyard. Outside the jetty, two draggers, nets hanging from the gallast frame at the stern, make their way up from Three Mile Harbor. Obviously they have heard of the action at Montauk as well.

We head for the Point, past Gin Beach, a long sandy flat that holds cruising bass in the summertime. Then Shagwong Point with its reef that leads to Oyster Pond Cove to the east—a natural funnel for bait and gamefish, much like Montauk Point. The shore is wild and undeveloped, a forest of scrub oak and pines and a fringe of beach plums and shore grass. All of the land between the village of Montauk and the Point was once common pasturage for the cows and sheep of the freeholders of East Hampton. We pass no houses, no marinas, just the end of Long Island as it has always been.

The remnants of a tropical storm are bearing in on us from the south so the most that we can hope for is a two or three hour window of fishing before the seas build too much for our small flats skiff. In the distance, we see a few boats in the tidal rip that has formed out past the lighthouse. That beacon was originally ordered up by George Washington in 1792, one of the first lighthouses built by the young republic. Years of wrecks and near wrecks made it a necessity for the growth of seagoing commerce. Washington figured that, given the rate of erosion at the Point, the lighthouse was good for about two hundred years, which worked out to a nice amortization of the $22,300 that Congress appropriated for the project. He was right about the erosion. Were it not for considerable shoring up and bulwarking, the Point would have retreated westward and tumbled the lighthouse into the sea years ago.

When we round the Point, there is a flotilla of boats of all sizes as far as I can see. A picket line of surfcasters ranges along the shore. Mobile homes crouch on the cliff tops like a row of pillboxes. Those cliffs, and the rocky rubble on the ocean floor (carved out of them by the elements), extend all the way to Montauk Village. Here and there a house stands on the bluff, but on the shoreline itself there is nothing for six miles until the white beaches start at the Village and run all the way to Brooklyn a hundred miles to the west. Rocky shore and sweeping tides like Montauk's are excellent habitat for bass and other inshore gamefish largely because bait find it congenial as well.

A big charter boat nearly twice our size cuts across our path, its engines rumbling deeply. Three fishermen, big and heavy set, each hold on to a rod in one hand and the side of the boat in the other as they bounce through the rip, trolling lures. This kind of fishing is as much like flyfishing as butterflies are like bacon. No matter, Amanda waves and smiles.

No response.

She waves again and grins.

"You just won't let them not wave, will you?" I remark. "You're like Davy Crockett grinning a raccoon out of a tree."

"Why not? People get so goddamned serious and turfy. Me, I am determined to get along with everybody. I won't let them get me mad. I just wave until they wave back. That means I win."

Just then a dozen snapper blues (young of the year) leap from the rip. Amanda kills her engines and picks up her rod. She is a lefty who learned her flyfishing on salt water, so her cast has none of the frantic to and fro that betrays trout fishermen who begin saltwater flyfishing after years on the stream. She has a sense that there will be fish here and not there, that a cast in the next second but no later than five seconds from now will catch a fish, that if she cuts the engine right now and glides toward shore, she may ease up on a feeding school of tranquil stripers. I have been fishing way longer than she has. I have fished many more places. Occasionally I can cast farther. Still, time after time—so many times that I know it's not an accident—she has taken three fish to my one, four fish to my none.

A pod of albacore comes up in back of us. In unison, we wheel and fire, like grouse hunters pointing and shooting at the sound of flushing birds. Amanda is quicker than I. As the fish swirls, she connects with operatic enthusiasm.

She points her rod at the front of the boat and, looking like a terrified water skier holding on for dear life, runs forward, around the bow and then back to the rear as the albie dashes for safety. Amanda tries to keep it from doubling her rod over and breaking it. When she has subdued the albacore, she leans over the gunwales, grabs the albie by the tail, unhooks it, and with a parting "good-bye" drops it in the water.

"Good, but not amazing," Amanda observes. "Let's head west and see what's happening."

We move out at full throttle. The warm southern wind feels like velvet. "One of the last T-shirt days," she adds contentedly. She waves to David Blinken, another flyrod guide. With his blond, surfer hair and his twin-engine, forest-green Contender, he is, from stem to stern, the image of a hot-rodding stud. He knows how to fish and he lets you know it. The former excuses the latter.

As we approach the cliffs just west of the Point, we see Paul

Dixon. He gestures to us and then to the water in front of him. There in the rocks next to the shore, a black mass churns the water. The bait leap into the air. I have heard it theorized that the bass use their tails to bang the bait, smacking the small fry into the air. Maybe so, but I think most of the fish are leaping out of the water because they are crazed with fear and nothing living wants to die today.

The feeding stripers are so tightly packed that there is no water in the spaces between them—in fact, there is no space. I know that bass are black and silver, but because of their writhing motion there is also, for some reason not apparent from the laws of optics, a greenness and darkness to the frenzy: It is as if a single living mass of color has come up out of the ocean. The bass, when they rise to the surface this way, become one sea creature.

I cast into the sea thing. I am a little short. A bluefish strikes— blues tend to hang outside the bass schools, opportunistically picking off stray baitfish. Five minutes later all eight pounds of him goes into the cooler. On the next pass, I take the helm and Amanda picks up her rod. Bang! A thirty-four-inch bass slams her fly. I back us out and she fights the fish to the boat, unhooks it, and releases it. Then Josh connects: two fish in short order. I catch. Amanda catches. Every approach produces a good bass.

"I'm keeping this one for dinner," I say as I heft a twenty-nine-inch fish into the cooler.

"Oh man !" She disapproves. Amanda is a catch-and-release angler, like most of the flyrod guides out here. I, too, am a conservationist but I am also a cook.

"Your dinner, Amanda."

"Yeah, well, whatever."

Other boats show up. The only way to fish this small pod of

big bass is for one boat to move in, hook up, and back out. It becomes a circle dance. We wait back from the pack. Providentially, a huge school of large bass blows up behind us. We circle and drift into them. Within two or three casts, Josh and I are into keeper fish. We land them. Amanda stands on the stern, spreads her arms wide and cracks a grin as wide as a pie plate.

"You can have a whole month of crummy fishing and then this!" she exults, referring to the August doldrums that are now officially ended.

We fish until we have our fill, and when we leave the bass are still working. Amanda and I make a date for dinner at my house at 8:00. I return to my new kitchen with its monster stove and acres of counter space. I put John Coltrane's *Ballads* on, open a cold beer, and start dicing.

Paul, showered and dapper in a crisp Hawaiian shirt, and Amanda, in a fresh T, show up on time. I pan roast the bass dusted with cornmeal and topped with a salad of diced tomato, watermelon, celery leaves and chili oil, a recipe that I learned from Gray Kunz, a gifted chef with whom I worked on a cookbook. The trick in this recipe is to season the fruit and vegetable combo seconds before serving so it stays crisp.

Any misgivings the anglers have about my keeping a bass are forgotten as they go back for seconds and thirds. I was pretty sure they would. Conservation, we agree, is an important policy, but not a religious dogma where one transgression lands you in sportsman's Hell.

"Is this it, Paul," I ask, "do you think this is The Run?"

"I figure it could be. It always starts out this way. The big fish are the early arrivals, usually a small school. This stands to reason. They're older, have been fished more. There are some mongo fish in there. Huge! Those big guys show up right after the rainbait move in. Then the other year classes of bass show up, usually smaller in size. As they congregate, you get bigger and bigger concentrations of fish. If the weather holds and the bait isn't blown way offshore, this is The Run."

We gab for a while, but since we are all going to be up early, we call it a night around 10:30. When they leave, I turn on my weather radio. A voice I'll learn to know well comes on the NOAA band. I call him the Irish Robot. His automated voice is, to my ear, a machine version of an Irish lilt. The weather should be fine tomorrow. I leave the curtains open. It lets me take in the view and the light wakes me up at dawn, which is when anglers are supposed to rise.

# The Salt Rush

≈

FISHING FOR LARGE and voracious predators in the trackless
ocean doesn't correspond to the common image of the flyrodder
as a tweedy, pipe smoking esthete, most often found on country
brooks. Saltwater flyfishing has changed that stereotype largely,
but not solely, because of the striped bass.

There was a time, as recently as ten years ago, when serious
flyrod anglers still lumped the bass in with other coastal gamefish
and thought of them all as big and stupid. However, as saltwater
flyfishing boomed, knowledge and techniques have also improved and one fish had to emerge as the heart's desire of the
flyrod angler. In all flyfishing, much depends on where and how
the fish is caught, what tactics you can employ and, ultimately
and indefinably, how much esthetic pleasure the quarry offers.
Finding it, casting to it, hooking it, fighting it and (most of the
time) releasing it all contribute to the overall esteem in which a
particular gamefish is held.

In the Northeast, the striper has become the saltwater edition
of the trout: a fish that you can study in a habitat that you can
learn to read, and with a way of showing itself by swirls, slurps,

whooshes and gulps that any flyrod angler will understand and lust after.

It's not as if the saltwater sport were just invented. A fair number of the flyfishing cognoscenti have pursued bonefish, tarpon and permit on the tidal flats of the Keys and the Bahamas since World War II. These semi-tropical fish offered the chance to flyfish in the non-trout months. In northern waters, in the '40s and '50s a few serious flyrod pioneers pursued the striper, among them the angler/author Joe Brooks, whose adventures foreshadowed much of the subsequent evolution of the sport. Apart from these prophets in the wilderness, however, the deep lore and mystique of flyfishing were still commonly held to belong to salmon and trout.

Then came the flyrod boom, engendered in part by Robert Redford's film version of *A River Runs Through It*. It looked so romantic, so cool. It had a New Age Zen component combined with the thrill of a blood sport: You could get that cave man high and then release your fish to grow up again. Very exciting, and very politically correct. Sometimes I think if flyfishing hadn't been around in the mid 1980s, someone would have invented it before the decade was out because it fit the cultural bill so well.

Blue-ribbon trout streams became more and more crowded, until finally flyfishermen (and increasing numbers of flyfisherwomen) forsook the long drives to overpressured streams. They began to spend more time on the salt water. They looked for a fish that satisfied the contemplative, soul-restoring aspects of the sport. Saltwater flyfishing became less of an afterthought and much more of a refined, challenging, full-blown angling art.

Credit this change in the prestige of saltwater flyrodding, in part, to full-time guides like Paul Dixon. As more and more salty flyrodders appeared, the sport acquired a critical mass of anglers who were ready and able to support full-time guides: people who could spend two hundred days a year on the water to learn new lessons and pass them on to their clients.

Equally to the point, the fishermen in the Hamptons and in similarly upscale Cape Cod, Martha's Vineyard and Nantucket had the money to spend on pricey equipment and thoroughbred guides. With this new sport, they didn't have to isolate themselves in the Maine woods for a week. Instead, they could have all the stress-draining diversion of flyfishing while spending time with the family and remaining plugged in to the happening social scene at the beach. For the overscheduled recreational angler, it was the right sport at the right time.

Dixon has been among its chief proselytizers. Now nearing fifty and having spent most of the last decade on the East End, he is a fair skinned, curly haired, Southern Californian with a quick laugh, a suave gentleman sportsman's manner, and an encyclopedic knowledge of every aspect of flyfishing gathered, as he often says, "from time on the water."

It was the striped bass that put Dixon on the angling map and, likewise, it has been the growth of the striped bass fishery that accounts for the explosion of interest in saltwater flyfishing in the Northeast. In fact while freshwater flyfishing is generally conceded to have peaked, the growth in saltwater flyfishing has been double digit for the last half dozen years.

In the warm months, Dixon poles the sandy flats hoping to come upon striped bass cruising placidly over white sands. They are as beautiful and unsuspecting as a herd of grazing impala. In the fall, when the bass leave the flats, he moves his boat from Three Mile Harbor, near the head of Gardiners Bay, to Montauk Harbor, close to the Point. The quiet and solitary fishing of the summer becomes the October rugby scrum at Montauk.

Many of the small group of flyrod guides on the Point started out working for Paul, handling his overflow. This year he took on Amanda Switzer, who fell for flyfishing the way Paul and I did years ago. Everything else in life comes in second by at least a few lengths. It is a religion she has come to by stages. First she fished conventional tackle with Dad, then, as a sideline to her own landscaping business, she would crew on tuna and shark boats. If you think a female flyrod guide is unusual, imagine that same woman knee-deep in shark and tuna gore. Think of her gaffing a mako and pumping a coup de grace into it with a .38.

Somewhere along the line, flyrodding intrigued her. She stopped in at Paul Dixon's former store, asked for advice on where to fish, and, all on her own, spent the next few years walking the shore on Gardiners Bay learning to cast, learning to read the water. When she felt she knew how to flyfish, she took her rod, went to Central America, checked into a cheap hotel, and fished every day for tarpon until she caught one on a fly.

This past year she ended her marriage and took a sabbatical from her landscaping business to sign on with Paul as a full-time guide. In so doing, she became the first woman flyrod guide at Montauk. Her looks, affability and angling prowess combined to make her the most notable newcomer at the Point.

Amanda, Paul and I would talk first thing in the morning, last thing at night. If fishing was involved, there was no wrong time to call. We traded updates all day, every day.

On the bass front, the main news in the first days of my stay was no news. Cooling temperatures will change that. The bait will move toward the Point and, all things being equal, stay there through October. The bass will grow hungrier in preparation for their migration and they will stay where the bait stays. So will I.

# The Perfect Storm of 1938

≋

THE RAIN DRIVES IN SHEETS against my bedroom window: gray sea, sallow sky, fog, rain, lashing wind, the dim outline of Gardiners Island. No fishing today. Gardiners Island, my constant landmark, has belonged to the Gardiner family since colonial times. The island was formerly called Manchonake, which translates to "Island of the Dead" (perhaps, it is thought, because the whiteman's diseases killed all of the Native Americans who lived there). It was purchased by Lion Gardiner, a soldier in the service of the colonial government in Connecticut who made peace with the local Indians. In recognition of Gardiner's service to the crown, the island was made a royal grant that established the family's right to it in perpetuity.

Because of the royal land grant, there is still some confusion among residents, particularly newcomers, about whether or not the Gardiners are British nobility. They are not, but their island remains a royalist anachronism, the perpetual property of the family as long they stay solvent enough to hold on to it. Smugglers and pirates, from Captain Kidd down to the rumrunners of Prohibition and their descendants in the cannabis trade, have occasionally found brief refuge there.

I won't be going near Gardiners today. Whitecaps and drenching rain have put a hole in everyone's fishing plans. It's good day for the library.

The documents in the local historical collection are housed in a wood paneled room with lots of space to spread out and take notes. The catalog has plenty of listings about commercial fishing, but comparatively few about recreational fishing. This is pretty true to form. The amount of money earned in the cod or herring fisheries is enormous when compared to the take for more sporting species such as swordfish or striped bass. The same goes for trout or the freshwater basses. Though we anglers are obsessed with them, there is relatively little written about them beyond sporting panegyrics.

I chance upon a collection of the *Long Island Fishing Guide*, an annual publication of the East End Surf Fishing Club, from the '30s and '40s, previously unknown to me. The journal is a hodgepodge of angling advice and fishing club gossip. Every year there is a "gee golly who woulda thunk it!" story about how one of "the gals" actually caught a swordfish, thereby putting "the guys" to shame. There are a considerable number of advertisements for lodgings and charters out of Greenpoint and Riverhead, largely because there was no sportfishing business to speak of in Montauk in the 1930s.

The 1941 edition has an illustration of a lovely young woman in a Betty Grable–ish two-piece pale green swimsuit. She casts into the breaking surf. Inside the journal, a fulsome editor's note introduces a piece by Ted Gusdanovic, who is described as "the most scientific fisherman to be found along any beach." The editor goes on to gush, "Without one bit of doubt, we assert that the surf fisherman will find more actual 'meat' concerning surf fishing in this article than in any other printed matter he has ever read. Read it and find out what you want to know!"

The experienced sportsman learns to take such claims under advisement. Nevertheless, Gusdanovic's description of surf fishing is a clear and accurate exposition of the effects of wind and tide through the year. I am particularly interested in what he says about the Autumn Run.

During the end of September and the first part of October, southerly or southwesterly winds mean excellent fishing for weakfish. Easterly winds are no good for this specie nor are they for the striped bass. These winds usually bring on high tides and heavy groundswells, and therein lies the reason. The beginning of October and southeast winds, mean good bluefish waters, if there are any bluefish around! Northeast winds, with or without rain are excellent for striped bass. Southwest winds can't be beaten for all types of fishing. In October, the fish are schooling for migration and the bait is starting to leave the bays and creeks. The proper place to fish at this time is in the tide rips or in the deep sluice ways along the beach or on an ebbing or rising tide where the wind traps the bait in the swirling waters. Once in a while, at the flood peak, in a rip tide when the bait is being driven to the surface, those precious moments may be worth more than several days ordinary fishing. You'll also find that the first heavy northwest blows during October mean excellent fishing. At this time the first large schools of striped bass show up. They will hit them, on a rising tide, regardless of the time of day. Although northwest winds presage excellent fishing at their beginnings, they cool the water rapidly, especially when they are interspersed by a few northerlies. More southwest winds and occasional winds from the southeast will mean warm water and longer fishing.

Things have not changed since 1941, at least in regard to autumn fishing: same wind, same tide, same fish.

I am keen to see the 1939 edition, because that was the one that followed the Great Hurricane of 1938. Of the five "epic" storms (Category 3 or higher) that have hit Long Island in historical times, it was by far the greatest. Judging from popular folklore—there were no scientific records in earlier times—the only two to rival it were the Great New England Hurricane of 1635 and the Great September Gale of 1815. Governor John Winthrop of the Massachusetts Bay Colony described the first tempest as "such a mighty storm of wind and rain as none living in these parts, either English or Indian ever saw. . . . It blew down sundry houses and uncovered others. . . . It blew down many hundred thousands of trees turning up the stronger by the roots and breaking the higher pine trees off in the middle."

The 1815 storm, another doozy, was memorialized by Oliver Wendell Holmes in a eulogy to his first pair of long pants, which were torn from the clothesline by "The September Gale":

*It came as quarrels sometimes do,*
*When married folks get clashing;*
*There was a heavy sigh or two,*
*Before the fire was flashing,*
*A little stir among the clouds,*
*Before they rent asunder,—*

*A little rocking of the trees,*
*And then came on the thunder.*

*Lord! how the ponds and rivers boiled!*
*They seemed like bursting craters!*
*And oaks lay scattered on the ground*
*As if they were p'taters*
*And all above was in a howl,*
*And all below a clatter,*
*The earth was like a frying-pan,*
*Or some such hissing matter.*

*It chanced to be our washing-day,*
*And all our things were drying;*
*The storm came roaring through the lines,*
*And set them all a flying;*
*I saw the shirts and petticoats*
*Go riding off like witches;*
*I lost, ah! bitterly I wept,—*
*I lost my Sunday breeches!*

Though those two storms were extremely powerful, even lethal, they did not approach the impact of the 1938 hurricane, which has come to be known as the Long Island Express. Apart from its great force, it is remembered for the way it descended on the Northeast without warning. Although meteorologists were aware of this Class 5 storm (the scale only goes up to 5), only one junior forecaster, Charlie Pierce of the National Weather Service, predicted landfall on Long Island and New England. He was overruled by his superiors, who issued a warning for an overcast with a possibility of rain.

The night before the hurricane hit Long Island, it was off Cape Hatteras, 611 miles to the south. Then the unpredictable and unprecedented happened. For those of us accustomed to watching the progress of hurricanes boiling up from the tropics, we are used to forward motion of the storm track at about 5 to 10 miles an hour. Not the Long Island Express. There must have been a true speed demon in the heart of this storm that sent it bouncing off the high pressure system to its east and tracking straight up the coast at 70 miles an hour. Remember, this wasn't winds of 70 miles an hour, *this was forward motion of a storm system 500 miles wide.*

Within the body of the storm, the meteorologist at the Blue Hill Observatory, Charles F. Brooks, recorded winds of 186 miles per hour, the highest ever at that station. He wrote in the Congressional Record of January 19, 1939:

This vortex rushed northward to Long Island and New England with the speed of an express train, augmenting wind velocities to extremes of about 120 miles an hour of the east to the path of the center. The wind drove the sea water with such force that, when added to the rise in sea level due to a low pressure and thrown against the coast, the sea rose 10 to 15 feet above the expected level, in itself high water, the time being high tide. Towering surges of this combined astronomical tide and storm wave threw the sand to such heights the demolition was general along the exposed coast and hundreds of persons were engulfed and drowned. Flying spray encrusted windows and salt killed the vegetation 20 miles inland and traces were found even 50 miles from the raging sea.

When the Long Island Express hit the coast, it made landfall during one of the highest tides of the year. Waves of 30 to 50 feet spilled over the dunes. On an audiotape given to me by Montauk conservationist and offshore angler Bill Aiken, Gus Pitts, one of the early charter boat captains out of Montauk in the 1930s, recalls the day the storm hit.

This guy comes over and tells my wife, "There's a hurricane coming Mrs. Pitts." She says, "Oh, let it come." She didn't know what a hurricane was anymore than I did. It started from the south, then the eye was still and then it turned around and came back again, in a circle. That's what really done the damage. If it hadn't been for the Long Island Railroad, I'd say 100 people would have drowned. [You see] the track was six feet higher than the beach and when all of these women with their children saw the water was coming over the beach they ran for the train and they got on board the train and the train took them out of the cold. It stayed there. I was on the lake (Lake Montauk) and I saw the tidal wave coming over the jetty. My father was there so I asked him what was he going to do. He said that he was going to stay down there and see what was going to happen. One puff of wind took his car right up in the air; he never did find it. He hung on to a telephone pole. I jumped in my car and I came up to the bay here and I rescued my family. I rescued my sister and her husband and Buddy and Emily, my dog, Edna Steck and my two aunts and we started for Montauk Manor and that's where we stayed.

The havoc was enormous. Montauk Harbor was destroyed and with it a hundred boats in the fleet, effectively destroying the sportfishing business for years. Shinnecock Inlet and Moriches Inlet, two major features of the south shore of Long Island, did not exist until this storm scoured them out. Even so, Long Island got off relatively lightly. The south coast of New England was completely devastated and the final death toll was six hundred.

Given the epochal nature of the event, I turned with interest to the *Long Island Fishing Guide* to get a firsthand feel from on-the-scene anglers. Writing the "President's Message" for the 1939 edition, which covers the events of 1938, George W. Hildreth reported,

> Nineteen thirty-eight was memorable in the history of the club. Chief among important events was Ladies' Night at Canoe Place Inn last May. There were over five hundred present and prizes aggregating $250 were distributed among the ladies. Ladies' Night will be repeated at the same place this year.

That's it, no notice taken of the hurricane. Charles Pierce, the junior forecaster who was the only person who called it right, was promoted to the rank of forecaster the next year. He spent the remainder of his career with the National Weather Service.

Part Two

MR. OCTOBER

# October 1: Swells

≋

THE IRISH ROBOT GIVES the progress of three hurricanes heading up the coast: George, Isaac and Keith. He says their names as if they were three heart-throbby members of a boy band. This is confounding to me. Before storms had cuddly first names, they held more dark mystery. Properly so, I think. Storms are chaotic, anarchic, dangerous, beautiful. Sit by the sea when even the most piddling tempest is brewing, and you don't think about cutesy George or Isaac or Keith. You think about God, or Neptune, or at least a big Mahler symphony. You think of yourself caught in the waves and about to go down. Nature doesn't have a first name and if she did, it would not be Keith.

The Robot does not predict much to worry about in the way of a direct hit from one of these storms. They are headed for other parts. "A strong storm of very large proportions [Isaac] is headed for Chetumal Bay," he says, pronouncing the Central American estuary *chedd-a-mull*, as if it were a curry.

The storm in Chetumal will miss us but the waves that it whips up will build across a thousand miles of ocean until they break on the Long Island shore. The Robot predicts swells of 4

...eet off Montauk. Although waves and swells look the same ... a surfer or a boater, they are not the same thing. A wave is an undulation in the ocean created by wind. A swell is what happens when that undulation travels beyond the reach of the wind. It is the effect of a wind far away.

The forecast is for winds at a placid 2 miles an hour, but the big swells have convinced Amanda to pull the plug on our first trip of October. When those swells come up from the south and the outgoing tide meets them under the lighthouse at Montauk, the ocean gets very big, very quickly, and every year some angler entranced by the fishing in front of him, instead of the tumult all around him, drowns, or nearly does.

Josh Feigenbaum and I decide to drive to the north-facing beaches. They will be protected from the wind. Josh asks me to meet him at the bagel shop in Amagansett. I have never put the words "Amagansett" and "bagel" in the same sentence and I have never been to the bagel shop, which is why I drive right past it. By the time I find it, our appointment time has passed. Has Josh been and gone? Probably not. In the twenty-five years that he and I have fished, I have never known him to be on time.

Josh and I became friends when we both worked at *Rolling Stone* magazine in 1971. He has the same full head of dark curly hair that he had then and the same beefy college wrestler build. He was a salesman. He went on to build an enormous radio company and I cannot tell what makes him more proud: the fact that he never wore anything but chinos and sneakers to work for twenty-five years, or that he cashed out this year with enough money to fish whenever and wherever he wants. In business he is a tiger, in friendship a pussycat.

Josh and I have fished through girlfriends, marriages, divorces, births, deaths, graduations, cross-country moves, bad movies, big bottles of burgundy, blowhard clients. I can call Josh anytime and suggest fishing and he will probably take me up on it.

Like any long-term relationship, ours has its strains. The biggest one is getting out in the morning. Josh is one of those shower-before-you-go-fishing guys. I am from the pull-your-pants-on, grab-a-candy-bar-and-get-out-the-door school. Somehow we have maintained our friendship in spite of this.

I have made it through most of *The New York Times* and a bagel with salmon spread by the time Josh pulls up.

"Let me get a bagel and a coffee," he says by way of greeting, which means another ten minutes before we get on the road. Come to think of it, so what? It isn't going to affect our fishing. I am just antsy and raring to go.

We stop by Harvey Bennett's store for his report on likely beach spots. Harvey, a Vietnam veteran, sports a bandana headband and runs a bait and tackle store on the highway between Amagansett and Montauk. He says he plans to vote for Hillary Clinton *and* Pat Buchanan. The Bennett family is thirteen generations old in the East End, all the way back to the arrival of the Gardiners. It is one of a handful of families whose name pops up in any fishing annal of the area.

In what was determined to be a "hunting accident," Lion Gardiner's grandson, also named Lion, was gunned down by Harvey Bennett's great-great-great-great-grandfather (give or take a handful of greats). Harvey says the shooting was over a woman. He takes it as a sign of his peacemaking skills that he is now allowed to overnight on the Island during waterfowl season although he steers clear of the cemetery where his ancestor's victim rests.

When Josh and I greet him, Harvey launches into a pungent

discourse about the aggravating sense of entitlement of some of the newcomer flyrod guides. It is a sore point among the natives, especially ones like Harvey, who was one of the first guides to book flyrod trips. If it were a rainy day, we could spend hours at Harvey's and he would fill the time with stories and opinions. Since fishing is back on the agenda, though, we take the opportunity to wish Harvey good-bye when he stops his story to take a phone call.

We receive a call at the same time. It's Paul. Through the static his message is clear. "Get Amanda and get out here. We have fish."

We head for Amanda's. She lives not far from my house, but that area is such a labyrinth of back roads that Josh and I are hopelessly lost within minutes. We probably would have missed her had Amanda not been waiting in the road with her flyrods.

When we finally leave the harbor, the sun is bright. The air is soft. The wind is down. We move out of the harbor, past Gin Beach. Bass are not in the cards today. We are after albacore because albacore are what's happening. Though I prefer bass, I am not doctrinaire. You fish for what is fishable.

There are many anglers who make the trip to Montauk just for the albies. Though the speed and strength of these fish are impressive, a steady diet of them is not my idea of great flyfishing. But every now and then, on a day when the bass are not cooperating, they are just the ticket.

By the time we reach Shagwong the outgoing tide has carried the schools of bait further toward the Point. The tide and the opposing swells make for a heaving rip tall as a line of low hills. At least fifty boats work the tumultuous water. I recognize many of them: David Blinken's green Contender, retired NYPD detective Jim Levison's Parker, Ernie French's SeaCraft.

As we near the Point, Amanda sees a school of bait.

"Look, there, at two o'clock," she directs. Fly fishermen, like fighter pilots, call out the location of their quarry by their position on the face of an imaginary clock, with the prow of the boat as 12:00.

I look but see nothing until the bait breaks the surface and shortly after the albacore plough through the school.

"Fire," Amanda directs again. We try to get off a cast but the school is down within seconds. This will be a day of quick casts and fast reflexes if we hope to catch anything.

There was a time, just a few years ago, that we all thought you needed to cast quickly and move the fly just as quickly in order to hook albies. Moving over this same rip in 1993, Paul, Josh and I would speed after schools. One of us would lie belly down on the bow of the boat. As we approached a school, the angler would rise, and attempt to fire off a cast before our bow wave disturbed the school. When the fly hit the water you stripped like hell, retrieving it hand over hand. The thought was that the albacore were up and down so quickly that one had to move one's fly with equal speed.

We rarely caught a fish this way. Dixon was the first angler I know to realize that once the swift albacore had the bait penned up, they moved through *slowly* in order to maximize their time amidst the greatest concentration of food. Therefore, although everything about the albacore suggests speed, successful angling calls for moving the fly slowly, keeping it in front of the fish for a longer period of time.

We see Paul's boat on the rip that extends from Montauk Point on toward the seaward side of Gardiners. You can't miss his SeaCraft. With its deep vee, it is built to move through the waves and rips of the fall. If a flats skiff is like a stiletto, this is more of a well balanced and hefty sabre. It says "HAMPTON'S FLYFISHING TEAM" in big block letters on its side. This is great advertising for Hampton Watercraft Marine, who gave Paul the boat. It is not an unalloyed blessing, however: When you are thought by your peers to have special fish-finding gris-gris you would just as soon have the ability to sneak off without attracting attention. When Paul moves, he often takes the fleet with him.

He has two clients on board: Steve Byers, my former editor at *Men's Journal* and *Outdoor Life,* and Peter Matthiessen, the author whose book *Men's Lives* chronicles the baymen of the East End. These baymen—clammers, scallopers, fishermen, hunters and setters of the traditional haul seine nets on the south beaches—are the last of the hunter-gatherers in this part of the world.

The alarum of conservationists and sportsmen succeeded in pushing through legislation that has outlawed haul seining. In my opinion it was not a necessary law. True, the haul seiners harvested fish right next to the beach, but their take was pissant in comparison to the thousands of tons of fish netted by the big trawlers. Probably the worst count against the haul seiners is that they were visible from the beach-front homes of the arriviste city folk who came out here after 1970.

At seventy-five, Matthiessen has a lean and athletic build. He wears a khaki shirt, a long-brimmed hat and well-aged khaki pants. He has never caught an albacore on a fly. Dixon is jazzed to have him on board. In the green swells, their boat rises above us one moment, and dips below us the next. The foam on the choppy seas slides down the face of the waves.

The rip is alive with albacore. They come up and go down within thirty seconds. The fleet chases them with little success.

With everyone flitting to and fro, we are left relatively uncrowded.

We are near Paul, working on the same school of fish. While Josh makes a call, something he does with great frequency, Amanda picks up a rod. The candy cane shape that her flyline forms is long and narrow. Anglers call it a tight loop. It's what you want to cut through the wind and deliver the fly at a distance. With the heavy rods and lines used on salt water, a long slow casting stroke like hers is best. If you grew up trout fishing it looks like a slo-mo cast. It is something I will have to work on. Amanda has it down to a tee.

Amanda false casts only once and releases the fly into the middle of the feeding fish, right where one just boiled. The albacore takes. "Goddamn," she says triumphantly and leans into the fish, letting it feel the full force of the rod. She brings it to hand quickly, but when she leans over to grab it, she almost breaks her rod as it streaks off on another run before surrendering.

The *Marlin V*, a party boat with a full load of eighty or ninety anglers, makes its way toward us. It is big and ungraceful, moving from side to side in the swells like a fat baby who has just learned to walk. The anglers on board wave to the smaller boats. The albacore go down and stay down until the wake of the *Marlin* disappears. I think that fishing etiquette would have them make a circuit around our smaller boats but the captain has an I-was-here-years-before-the-rest-of-you attitude. No one gets too worked up about it. When there is enough bait and enough fish nobody stays mad.

Josh returns to the bow. I'm in the stern. He steadies himself against the waist-high rail that Amanda, like most guides, has put on the front of the boat for the fall fishing. Without it, many anglers would no doubt pitch overboard in the autumn waves. I prop myself against the poling platform.

Paul starts to move over to say hello when the school busts right in front of us. I false cast and let fly. Bingo! Mr. Albacore eats. It feels good to do that with an audience.

After we release the fish I remember that I have promised my wife, Melinda, that we will be back in time to spend part of the day together (she and my daughters come out on weekends). We have a longtime understanding that I will be home when I say I will be home *unless* the fishing is spectacular. In that case it is understood, in the words of an Ozarks watercolorist with whom I once fished, "I'll be home at dark-thirty."

We catch a few more fish. The tide finishes and it will be another hour before we have moving water again. When the water doesn't move, the bait disperses and so do the gamefish. We could chase the tide further west, but that is usually productive on the south side and we don't have the seas to venture there safely. We call it quits.

Amanda drops us off at the Crabby Cowboy. Now that she has the afternoon off from guiding she is going back out to fish. Josh and I stop in at the seafood market in the shopping center just east of Amagansett. Usually a store in a modern, low-ceilinged, fluorescent-lit, strip mall screams to me "Don't buy anything here." But here between the bay and the ocean, five miles from the harbor and the fishing fleet, the fish is glistening and fresh in a way you never see in New York. True, we have great fish markets in the city, but not all the varieties of local fish fresh off the boat—this is something even big-city dollars cannot buy.

There is pale pink toro—the belly meat of giant bluefin tuna. They run off of Block Island at this time of year. Their flesh is almost translucent and rich with oil that gives it an inviting sheen. There's tautog, or blackfish, in chunky white heaps. Huge fillets of striper are piled high on a metal tray in the ice chest. Small flounder, maybe a hundred of them, have the flecks of gray on their surface that mean they are as fresh as can be. We buy a dozen flounder fillets.

Melinda has made oven-roasted tomatoes with fresh thyme, salt, pepper and garlic. Every year we do fifty or sixty pounds of tomatoes when they are at their ripest and sweetest. That supply carries us through a lot of winter dinners. The flavor of the tomato in early autumn is intense, almost smoky. Roasting concentrates it even more. We serve the tomatoes with corn kernels fresh off the cob, breaded fish and crumbled bacon. A quarter cup of white wine, too, to bring out the bright tangy tomatoes, and a fortissimo dose of ground white pepper.

The maples have begun to flame and it looks like fall, but I am in no hurry for cold to arrive: sitting in the sun for a mindless lunch hour, watching the boats go by, I pray to whatever gods take an interest in flyfishermen: "Oh summer afternoons, stick around a while!"

# Monday, October 2:
# Right Where They Should Be

≈

PAUL CALLS JUST BEFORE 7:00 A.M. Sunday's golden afternoon has become a gray misty morning. The wind has turned around northeast. That should knock down the swells a bit—grand fishing weather, but Paul's clients have canceled out at the last minute. This, of course, means that Paul will take the opportunity to fish himself. I jump at his invitation.

We pick up sandwiches at The Springs General Store. Paul gets the same thing every day—turkey and mustard on a roll. To that order, I add two Hershey bars with almonds for that mid-morning sugar crash that fishing always brings on. The brown shingled store, the friendly Ecuadoran girl behind the counter, the clientele of writers, fishermen, gardeners and carpenters—I love the feel of any place where locals get their morning paper, their cup of coffee, their egg sandwiches.

Today marks my first ride in Paul's SeaCraft. The fishing is the same drill as yesterday, albies working the rip at the Point. Jim Levison, the ex-NYPD detective turned flyrod guide, is out with Peter Chan and his brother. There is no man alive who gives off more of a vibe of being at peace while fishing than Peter does. With his red bib overalls, black sweater and wide-brimmed hat, he has the air of a straw-hatted painter enjoying a tranquil landscape.

He greets me. He is fishing a spinning rod. I have seen him with one before on the jetty at Breezy Point in the Rockaways when he used to clamber over the treacherous boulders to the end where the albies were. I took a fall there one year, bashed up my casting arm and counted myself lucky that I didn't go into the rip. The next day I decided I had made my last trip to the end of that jetty.

Paul lets go a back cast into the feeding albacore. It is a smooth gesture that starts with a traditional flycast, body sideways and face forward, like a baseball pitcher. As he false casts, Paul turns his head to look backward, like that same pitcher checking a runner on second base. He releases the cast behind him and just as he does this, pivots his body and then moves his legs so that he is facing in the same direction as the cast.

Paul hits the boil of an albacore. He hooks up. Just then another school surfaces near me and I get off a cast swiftly enough to entice a fish. We race around the boat following our fish. Paul lifts his rod and I go under it. I do the same for him in a dance that goes on for five minutes until we have our fish in.

With two albacore on the scoreboard, there is no longer any danger that our boat will be fishless today, so that concern is laid to rest. The swells on the south side are big, but not so fearsome as yesterday so Paul cranks up and we run west another mile beyond Caswell's Point to where the cliffs descend to a low bluff. The houses that make up Andy Warhol's old compound sit there empty.

"Must have been some extreme parties there, Paul," I say with the undertone of envy that all semi-respectable people have about decadent folk and their dissolute gatherings.

"The way it's all isolated and out of the way. Man, they could do anything!" Paul concurs.

We drift a bit. The water is a soft gray blue. The birds aloft look clearly interested. There must have been something underneath the waves that agitated the bait. We drift behind the breakers. The push from the swells of the last few days raises them high and they take a long time to collapse. Seen from behind, their motion puts me in mind of a very tired person standing in front of a bed, swaying for a second and collapsing.

Paul casts a sinking tip shooting head—a dense heavy piece of flyline, no longer than thirty feet, with some lighter, limper line behind it. The idea is to get the heavy part beyond the guide tip of the rod and, if your casting physics are right, you will cast very far and the line will sink very fast.

Paul's fly hits the water. He counts one-Mississippi, two-Mississippi, until he thinks the fly is on the bottom. Then he strips in the line, hand over hand. On every third or fourth strip there is slight hesitation in his motion.

"You have to suck them up," Paul says. This is a term he uses to describe his technique of enticing a bass up from the bottom. I mimic it, but he tells me that I don't quite have it. Like most things in flyfishing, it will take a lot of practice, and mistakes, before I understand how this retrieve is supposed to feel.

On Paul's third cast he comes tight against a big bass. His rod bends double and the fish fights back, tearing line like a bluefish or an albacore, but the shakes of the head, the dips and feints of its struggle, are pure bass.

I see a swirl and cast. A pugnacious bluefish slams my fly, jerks my rod and takes off for deep water. What bluefish lack in finesse, they make up for in brute force. Then the inevitable happens as it always does when you fish for big blues without wire leader next to the fly. The bluefish bites through the nylon and is gone.

I wait for Paul to land his fish—a fat bass. "Best sizzle I've had this year," he says. "That's a good sign."

We see flocks of birds working in the distance, back toward the Point. Their tight formations, the way they ball up and dive, indicates a serious concentration of gamefish. Paul opens the throttle wide and the boat gets up on plane as we throw caution to the wind and waves and chase the birds.

They move to the north side, just under the lighthouse. Like the birds, the surfcasters are clustered together too.

"When you see birds and surfcasters in the same spot, something is happening," Paul says, giving voice to what I instinctively know. "Let's wait."

Like a mirage that reveals itself to be no mirage but the real, longed-for thing, we see the birds turn and wheel at *something* near the rocks right under the lighthouse. The water turns brown, then brownish-red. The rainbait erupt. Then, right behind them, frothing, feeding fish. Stripers! Black and silver, Gestapo colors. They porpoise, showing head and tail as they move through the bait. Their sound is the roar of a distant crowd cheering.

A thousand stripers break in the foam under the lighthouse. The casters on the shore don't see them yet. They are still looking at where the bass used to be, not where they are now. The bass move through the bait in unison. This is what we have been waiting for but we cannot get to the fish yet without foundering.

The school goes down. It surfaces back in the cove where the surfcasters stand. The fishermen run to the spot where they will have the shortest cast. They hook up. Their catcalls and happy whoops punch through the sound of surf and the feeding herd of bass. Still we cannot approach. I feel like I am home from school with the flu and all my friends are playing baseball in the warm spring sun right outside my window.

"The rocks aren't quite as dangerous where the bass are now, but I don't want to move into range of surfcasters," Paul explains. "It isn't fair and it pisses them off: These guys are confined to their spot while in a boat we can move quickly to where the fish are. And if you don't buy the fairness argument, wait till one of these guys sends two ounces of lead at your face. There are some casters there who can reach out pretty far and they can cast accurately. Give it time. The fish will move out to us with the tide. We wait."

The fish move, but only teasingly. We still cannot get to them. The albies come up just on our side of the last breaker. Paul backs the boat in on them, ready to pull out in a hurry if a big wave pushes us onshore.

We catch albacore, looking over our shoulders as we do to see what is happening with the bass. Next to us there is a small yellow boat from Connecticut. We have seen the two guys in it running around for the last few days. They are broadside to the incoming swells, oblivious to everything but the fish around them. They come closer and closer to the last breaking swell. I am about to scream a warning when their boat lifts into the air and disappears behind a wave. I close my eyes, grit my teeth and scrunch up my shoulders the way you do when you step into a cold shower. I don't want to see this. The half-dozen boats fishing the rip all stop. We look until the wave subsides. We see the little boat no more than a yard from the rocks. The wide-eyed driver of the boat frantically turns the wheel, guns the motor and heads straight into the next oncoming wave. He rises over the top and, airborne for a moment, slides down its back face. He lands on the safe side of the breakers.

"Keep your bow pointed out," Paul yells. "You get a wave coming over your stern and you're going to take on water and go straight into the rocks and there is not a thing you can do about it."

"Right," they say as they mindlessly speed to another school of albacore. They have a severe case of fishing rapture. Like a dog chasing a tossed ball, they go here, they go there, go . . . go . . . go.

Some of the boats that have been fishing around us move further out in the rip as the tide takes the bait and with it the albacore. But Paul stays on the Point.

"That pod will move off and then we're going to be in bass. It may take an hour, it may take two hours, but we are going to catch bass."

We wait. The bass come closer. I see the ocean darken. Then the bass rise. It is as if a piece of the world has come alive—mysterious as sex, wet as a wound. In fairy tales, trees speak, mountains roar, the skies reveal spirits flying among the clouds. I don't believe in magic, but if I did, it would feel something like this. If only I could cast into it, hook up, and be connected to it. My line would be attached to the chaos and, for a moment, I would mainline the power of nature.

Finally, late in the afternoon, the black mass comes to us. The sound of tails slapping the water rises over the wind and the surf. We cast one of my favorite flies, Clouser's Minnow. With its lead eyes and its body of sparsely tied deer hair—usually with some sparkly synthetic material as well—the Clouser is the most versatile fly devised in the last two decades. It was invented for smallmouth bass by Susquehanna flyfisherman Bob Clouser, but it has been used to take bonefish, tarpon, bluefish, trout, striped bass. It is Dixon's fly of choice when the bass are massed together like this. If you cast a conventional fly without any metal weight tied into the head, it will just lay atop the backs of the bass. In contrast, the Clouser will slip off the bass and the lead will cause it to sink one or two inches, just enough to put it in front of the eyes of the feeding fish.

Every angling exercise—you can extend that to every art— has its ideal way of doing a thing. In a tightly bunched pod of fish you want your fly to land in the thick of it, right in the middle of the school. You can catch bass on the periphery, but it will just as often be a bluefish or an albacore. In the center, though, there will be bass so tightly packed, the silver in their sides disappears: they become serpentine blackness.

I cast and strip my fly slowly. A bass hits with a short jolt. Paul sticks a bass too. We fight our fish and drift away from the feeding pod. They move back into the wash of the breakers out of our reach. We follow them. I see something breaking in the water. It isn't bass: We are too close to the surf casters. Their lead weights land right in front of us. Paul backs out.

"The fish will stay in this tight to the shore until the tide changes," he promises.

Like someone darting close to a fire to throw in a stick and then retreating when the heat of the flames becomes too intense, the few flyrod boats attempt to approach the pod as close to shore as possible. The curses of the surfcasters, the nearness of the rocks, the protocol of hooking a fish and letting the next boat in, have us all approaching and retreating in formation.

For forty-five minutes we catch fish after fish, all of them keeper size. This is the real thing. A trout fisherman dreams of June, the hatch of the green drake mayfly, big as a Spanish doubloon; it pulls all the big fish up to the surface. In the Florida Keys, May is the time to be there as hundreds of thousands of tarpon head for Key West to eat the little red palolo worms that hatch out of the coral. The scene is like a trout pool, except these fish are the size of a trophy deer. At that time of year, the bonefish and permit that people spend thousands of dollars pursuing three months earlier become an afterthought, out of style, off the radar screen, not worth it. When an angling event happens—and this usually means the appearance of a particular prey—then that one thing is all you want to do.

Fishing a bass blitz is what I want to do at Montauk; it is *all* I want to do. Mayhem and fish. No angler could leave this. Top of the world, Ma.

# October 3: A Lone Eagle

≋

I HAVE BEEN ON A BOAT, fishing hard in big seas for two days. When I climb out of bed, I feel it in every part of my body. My hips hurt from banging into the bow rail. My thumb hurts from pushing the cast on a big saltwater flyrod. My neck hurts. Under the right conditions, flyfishing is a contact sport.

I make two brisket sandwiches, one for me and one for Jim Clark. I cooked the meat last night, a brisket the way my grandmother made it: smothered in onions, garlic and carrots, lathered with ketchup, mustard and ginger, seasoned with salt and pepper, and baked, covered, in the oven for nearly three hours. Grandma was of the school, and all great chefs concur, that you need to brown the meat really well. Browning means brown, not a light tan. Step one in her recipe was to brown the meat with onions until you could smell them burning in the store one flight down. She kept a grocery store in Kearney, New Jersey, at the end of the Jersey meadows, so this timing was a natural, if personal, one for her to give. I make the sandwiches on hard rolls I bought this morning at The Springs store. They are filled with juicy meat, onions, garlic, horseradish and sliced pickle.

Jim, a retired schoolteacher in East Hampton, is a big man

with the same Julius Caesar hairline that he had when I met him fifteen years ago. He was the first person with whom I flyfished on the East End. Now sixty-five years old, he is still fit, largely from kayaking almost every day (including the winter) on Gardiners Bay.

It is a warm, beautiful morning. The wind is west at a light 6 to 10 miles per hour when Jim pulls up to my house trailering a kayak. He made it himself. He is a great craftsman who must have some Shaker genes in him (which would make him the descendant of celibates). Everything he builds has such clean lines and beautiful finish. For a time he made doll's houses of a saltbox design, large ones, where all the windows opened and closed and the shingles were laid one by one on the roof. I remember my daughter Lucy marveling at one when she was three.

"I saw a very big bass last night," he tells me. "I swear it was forty inches. I was kayaking at nightfall and it leaped clear out of the water. Of course, I didn't have my rod with me." On the strength of that, rather than putting in at Gerard Drive, where I had yet to see a bass, we decide to drive around Accabonac Harbor to the spit of land where Jim kayacked last night.

On the way, Jim, who is a native bonacker, as the original settlers of the East End are called, launches into conversation as if he were picking up on a point that we were discussing a few minutes ago. Never mind that our last conversation was ten years ago. He tells me that his great-aunt Nellie lived just up the road from my house.

"My uncle Asa was Nellie's husband. In order not to work for someone else, they clammed, they shellfished. He had his garden, some ducks and chickens. He split wood."

"In the Ozarks they call it getting by, Jim, not working for somebody. Very important."

When we arrive at Barnes Landing, I help Jim with his kayak and then one-hand my canoe down to the water. We paddle out a short distance. With his silver hair, sharp-looking shades, faded denim shirt and salt-bleached baseball hat, Jim looks like an AARP poster boy. The breeze pushes us along so that all that is required of us is an occasional stroke with the paddle to keep us in formation, casting as we go. Moses in his basket in the reeds could not have had a gentler ride. Wind is so often your enemy in flyfishing that when it decides to push you so sweetly and when it gives your cast a confidence-building boost you want to say to it, "Why can't you always be this nice?" But it will do no good. Even when wind is your friend, it is your schizo, manic friend.

We drift gently and cast easily. Casting and fishing, especially when nothing is happening on the fishing end of things, is very conducive to conversation. There is a rhythm to such angling conversations. You can say something and the other person can let it hang there for thirty seconds before answering. In other circumstances this might be rudeness or absent-mindedness. In fishing it is as if each time you speak, the thing that you say sits there like a piece of bait or a lure or a fly. It has done its job when the other person responds, but that does not have to be right away.

We take a break to eat our sandwiches in the warm sun.

"Did I tell you about the eagle I saw this summer?" Jim asks with the air of somone rummaging through a stack of notes and seeing something that jogs his memory.

"I was paddling over by Water Fence [near Napeague] when a gigantic bird went up. I had never seen anything so large. It was a golden eagle. I could only get within sixty yards of her, and every time I did she would take off. So I kept paddling and she kept taking off to get a good distance between herself and me. Every time she landed she started pulling on something. It may have been a rabbit; you could see the entrails being pulled out. It wasn't a fish; it was a small mammal of some kind. She went up about six times as I paddled down the beach before she decided to lose me."

That's the end of the narrative. Jim doesn't tell beginning-middle-end stories. They are more like verbal snapshots. Hearing about a golden eagle, told in Jim's quietly marveling style, well outweighs the need for a story to come to a point, because the point is there was an eagle and he saw it and he shared what he saw.

We have passed the spot where Jim suprised his big bass. There are albies working way out in the bay. We chew and talk and watch for the fish to come in; it's too long a paddle to get to them. Finally, we return to the car and decide tomorrow we will try Montauk. Getting Jim to Montauk takes some convincing. Most of the locals I know avoid the crush at Montauk in the fall.

"It's always a long drive in the boat and the fish are never there," he says.

"Trust me," I counter.

When Jim leaves me at my house, I sit down to write but after an hour I give up. The day is too nice. I call Paul and Amanda. They are with clients at the tip of Gardiners Island. Apparently the ocean is still too rough at the Point: one of the cutely named tropical storms has sent the biggest swells so far. However, the albacore are in force on Bostwick Bay and Tobacco Lot (on the backside of Gardiners) so they should be there tomorrow, too. I know Jim will want to try that.

When flyfishing the ocean this time of year, a good rule of thumb is that if the fish are in a certain place on a certain tide, they will be there tomorrow as well, provided you correct for the hourly advance of the tides each day. For this reason guides, who are on the water every day, know where to go more often than the now-and-then angler does. Of course, the pattern will eventually change and the fish will go somewhere else and the guide will have to search them out. Count on this, though, if the fishing was good at some spot yesterday, anyone who knows that will be there today.

I stop in at Harvey Bennett's. They've been taking lots of bass everywhere on the beaches, he tells me. When a tackle shop owner gives you this news, you may allow for his verbal embroidery and still be sure people are probably catching something on the beaches. Of course, almost all of those fortunate anglers would be using conventional tackle. Whether or not the conditions are right for flyfishing is another matter.

I go directly from Harvey's store to the beach. The breakers are huge and booming, throwing spray twenty feet in the air. No way I can flyfish this water.

What I would like to do is sit on the deck and read while sipping a beer and eating potato chips. I have the reading matter, but I need the beer and chips. I stop at The Springs store and make right for the most larcenously expensive potato chips on the planet, the ones made with olive oil and rosemary. I first discovered them at Lake Placid and was shocked to find that they cost $2.99 for a bag. You can buy a dinner's worth of chicken parts for $2.99. But I love those potato chips and buy them even though they are $3.29 at The Springs store.

These particular potato chips will become my index of Hamptons Inflation. At the Amagansett Market, nearer to the beach and more expensive homes, the same chips cost $3.49. At the Sagoponack store, which is in the even more exclusive South of the Highway part of Bridgehampton, they are $3.99. The golden palm, however, goes to the Redhorse Market in the epicenter of priciness, just a short bike ride from Steven Spielberg's home in East Hampton . . . $4.39. In the Hamptons, in the summer of the Great Internet Bubble, prices and common sense inhabit two different worlds.

When Paul gets off the water, he calls. I tell him about the big bass that Clark saw at Barnes Landing. Paul has had a rough day with an unsatisfying client. An hour's fishing at sundown, just he, Amanda and I, sounds like the right antidote. We agree to meet at Accabonac Harbor. The tide should be moving so Paul reasons that if there are any bass left in the neighborhood, we will find them there.

We spread out along the beach just outside of the Neck, the same spot where I had come that first day on Gerard Drive. Where Amanda's casting stroke is long and slow, Paul's is longer and slower: curling, straightening, pausing, then reversing direction and repeating the sequence. Despite our efforts, Accabonac is a bust. We decide to try Devon, where Jim had seen the big fish. We arrive there in the dying light. Again, we spread out and cast as far as we can for as long as we like. The pure act of casting is the great joy in flyfishing. The catching is important, of course, but the thing that envelops you in the spirit of the angling moment is the casting. A well-executed flycast looks like the offspring of a ray of light and a gentle ocean wave.

Paul and Amanda fish Clousers. I cast a popping bug. When the sun is low, the sunset pink and the bay the color of weathered copper, the surface strike of a fish—bass or bluefish, it doesn't matter—is entirely delicious. I don't believe you can will these things to happen, but if you could, then my will and my gurgling popping bug would, at this moment, summon up a fish.

No fish. There are birds working over albacore by the black buoy a half mile offshore. If I had my canoe and it wasn't getting dark, I would row out there. But no canoe and night is falling.

At home, alone, I fry some bluefish, flake it and toss it with greens, lemon and vinegar. Sam Lester, a bonacker with whom I have surfcast for years, calls to tell me (or is that taunt me?) that he had fish on the beaches all day Friday and all day Sunday. I guess Harvey Bennett's claim about the hot fishing was more than tackle shop bravado. Sam couldn't go out this morning, because his reel mechanism was stripped from fighting all those fish. As best as I can tell through the telephone, he says this with a straight face. He may even have meant it with a straight face. Sam has some medical stuff to attend to. He tells me he will call when he's ready to fish again

Jim Clark had asked me about Plum Gut, a traditional bass hot spot that may have escaped the force of the incoming swells. I call Paul, who is still angry about his clients and needs to let off steam.

"We were fishing the Point but it was rough and there was no fish. I heard there were fish at Plum Island, so we drove there. The fish were busting all over there but these guys couldn't cast into the wind. In spite of that they caught fish but the wind got to them. They wanted me to find a lee. I warned them that you don't leave fish to find fish. I backed off to Bostwick Bay on the backside of Gardiners Island. There was nothing doing there. One of the guy says, 'Well, there's nothing happening. Let's go back to Rick's and have a margarita and meet a sixteen-year-old.' "

"Classy," I add.

He continues, "So I drop them at Rick's. Later, the guy calls his brother, who says he waited on the Point all day and caught four nice albacore the last half hour of the day—You know, the same time that you and I caught the bass yesterday, Pete—So he calls me up really disappointed that his brother got an albacore at the Point, and I get pissed because I put these guys on lots of fish and they caught fish. I tell him, 'I know for a fact that your brother waited there all day before they cast to one fish and you guys wanted me to go from Montauk and back and I did it.' I was so pissed I said, 'Look I don't want your business. I'll give you a list of ten other guides to call. Call them before you ever call me again.' "

Paul's diatribe is living, angry proof that when you deal with the public you are going to have some miserable people. When I drove a cab, my ratio of nice to horrible people was 1 to 3. Fishing is usually the reverse. I have found that when they are fishing, people are at their nicest, but even then you'll come across characters that infuriate you.

One piece of advice if you want to maintain this peaceful average, keep politics out of bounds in angling situations and you will up your chances of everyone remaining friendly. Even people with the sweetest dispositions can get nasty talking politics. It's useless too, because nobody ever changed another person's political point of view by talking about it—at least I have never seen it happen.

## October 4:
## Where Have All the Mongos Gone?

≈

THE ROBOT SAYS it'll be a nice day, about 70 degrees with north winds, 4 to 12. Paul is out early, so I check with him. He tells me that the Robot is wrong. The winds are out of the southwest and very light.

Jim Clark and I get under way within the hour. As we exit the harbor, the bluffs are frosted with daisies, dazzlingly white. The sky looks especially wide and big today: There are high clouds in the distance with God's fingers pointing through them to the sea.

We zip across the bay to Tobacco Lot on the seaward side of Gardiners Island. The albies are there. We drift over them but they are finicky. I see a large black shape out of the corner of my eye. For a moment I think it is the hugest striped bass in the world, but striped bass don't linger in the sun. I look again. It's a seal with a small flounder in its mouth. I hear its breath through its nose, like an old man carrying groceries to a third-floor walk-up. The albacore disappear. No fish wants to be around with a seal in the water. I know that Jim would prefer to stay here and catch fish far from Montauk, but we both take the seal as a sign . . . *go straight to Montauk!*

When we arrive, Paul is sitting off of the Point having a sandwich. He comes over to us.

"We're about to have a gam," Jim says.

"A what?"

"A gam. When two whaling ships meet at sea, they used to call it a gam."

"The bass were up strong, but they just stopped," Paul reports.

The anglers on the shore stand around, rods at the ready, hands on hips. They are attentive in the way that people are when something has just happened but isn't happening anymore. A between innings kind of look.

"There are albacore, outside," Paul says, indicating pods of fish here and there a quarter mile offshore. Some of the other boats chase them, but it's a very iffy thing. Here, close to shore, there isn't much depth to the water, so the only thing the rainbait can do to escape is to go up and stay up. Outside, they have forty feet of water under them. It is much easier to disperse, so the albacore rarely stay up. By the time you get to them they are down again. "I'm going west," he advises. "The tide will be moving and somewhere the bait will be trapped."

We follow along, cruising slowly. Just west of Turtle Cove I see the same four surfcasters on the same four rocks that they have been on for the last week. They wear wetsuits with ammo belts. On one side a knife hangs, and on the other a gaff. In a black body suit with dangling weaponry, a slim wetsuiter has a ninja look. A pot belly, which one of them has, kills the effect.

Typically they will wade out to a rock and stand there as the tide comes in. The occasional wave will knock them off. At times they will have to stay on their rock until the tide recedes enough to allow them to walk back. Hunter S. Thompson coined the term gonzo journalism to describe his reckless, out-of-control style of writing and researching a story. The wetsuit guys are gonzo fishermen.

They hurl their plugs with a swift crisp movement. None of that legato technique that old-timers like Sam Lester have artfully perfected. This is cast-and-slash fishing. Fight the waves, fight the fish, fight anybody who gets near your rock, fight the guys out there with their flyrods trying to get into "your piece" of water. Their plugs land seaward of the last breaker, right in front of me. Though the anglers are hard at work, the bass haven't started yet.

"What do we do now, Jim?" I ask.

"I don't feel like messing with albies. If I had a book I would say read a book until the bass show up . . . or try the Point."

Two of the wetsuit commandos connect. We watch them pump the fish in. Bass. They stand on their rocks, lift their fish, unhook them and toss them back in.

We motor back to the Point. Paul is there. Blinken, who had been chasing albies, is there too. Alex Powers, an elegant young angler with those long moves that make for fluid tennis players or easy swinging golfers, is tighter to the rocks than the rest of the pack. Even in this spot—where anyone at the wheel of a boat looks understandably nervous—he moves the boat with one hand and tosses off a backcast with a debonair flick. If a script had ever called for Fred Astaire to cast a fly-rod, it would have been with a move like Alex's. Ernie French, with two clients aboard, also glides in. Bob Sullivan, Wally Johnsen . . . in fact most of the Montauk flyrod fleet are here. The yellow boat with the men who almost wiped out two days ago joins in.

We drift over the inside rip, using one variation or another of the suck-'em-up technique that Dixon tried with success on our last outing. I have grown used to all the boats descending on a bass blitz. But now, with no blitz, they are on the Point because there are always fish here. However, the same currents that make it so productive as a fishery—the outflow of Gardiners Bay and Block Island Sound meeting the strong tides of the open ocean—also make for nerve-wracking boat handling. When there are many boats of different shapes, they catch the currents and spin and drift at different speeds. When there are many anglers—some looking, some fighting fish, some circling back around to start a new drift, some reacting to a forgetful moment that has brought them too close to a rock—it is a confusing traffic jam.

Jim and I take our place in this motorized water ballet. I hook a fish during my turn at the helm. I leave the engine running: That's bad form—it scares the bait. The fish sounds and I lean out to keep my line free of the prop, but the bass wants to go under the boat. I struggle to turn him. I can't. He wraps the prop. The flyline shears and fouls it. I have never done this before. Apart from being angry at myself and the fish, it is unmanning to foul up in full view of the fleet. We cannot even back out because we can't start the engine until the flyline is unwound from the prop. So, literally dead in the water, we drift through the mass of boats unable to give them room to fish. I feel like a hapless oaf.

"I can't stand this, too crowded, no fish, let's go," Jim says.

I am now deep enough into this thing that I know the blitz will happen in the next hour or so. I also know if we leave, there will be other days and that The Run will build. The best fishing lies ahead of me, I am sure, so I leave without protest.

Shortly after I return home, Vic Vecchio, a New York State

Department of Environmental Conservation scientist who specializes in the striped bass fishery, stops by my house for a beer. For the last twelve years Vic has conducted a haul seine survey of the striper migration. His crew are descendants of the old haul seine families. They are the last ones on the Long Island shore plying this ancient trade. Vic has invited me to visit his crew as many mornings as I would like. He usually starts his project on the first of October and continues until he has set and retrieved his net—a third of a mile long—forty-five times over the course of October and, if necessary, November.

Over the winter and spring, the nets have been mended, the boat and trucks are ready, as is the crew, but the swells of the past week have put the project on hold until the seas lie down. It is dangerous to launch a dory in heavy rolling ocean.

That there are any bass worth studying is one of the few and happy stories of a fishery that was given a second chance.

As with most marine resources, stripers were, until recently, treated as if they were a harvest-at-will species that would naturally replenish itself. Under the right circumstances that is true, but *only if enough* stripers are allowed to reach sexual maturity. When low size limits and unlimited bag limits led to a depletion of the stock, the Chesapeake fishery—by far the region's largest and the place from where most of our stripers come—nearly disappeared. In response, strict controls were put in place in 1986. The Chesapeake females were able to reproduce, sparking a dramatic comeback. In the Hudson, this policy had a halo effect, since Hudson River fish experience their greatest mortality from fishing pressure when they descend to the ocean in late spring (the same protected waters that the Chesapeake fish migrate to in the warmer months).

According to New York State Fisheries biologist Kathy Hattala, the effects of the stringent regulations were positively Malthusian: a skyrocketing bass population. Add to this the cleaning up of New York Harbor waters and with it the removal of the pollution block that kept young stripers from moving to nurseries in Jamaica and Raritan bays as well as the western Sound, and you have our current bumper crop.

"So how are we doing?" I ask Vic as we sit on my sun porch sipping a beer and munching on my expensive gourmet potato chips.

Vic answers in relatively plain English, but years of writing grants and reports and speaking at conclaves occasionally pushes his language into scientific governmentese.

"I would say we're doing very well. We have a lot of scientific data that leads us to think this, but it is not as if we are in a laboratory and can observe everything. What we do is called Black Box Statistics, because in the ocean, just like in a black box that you can't see into, you don't know exactly what's under the waters. You can collect samples and they give you statistics. The statistical theory is that over time, with enough samples, your random sample will approximate the actual distribution of bass. But you still really don't know for sure—as in you can look and see and count—what's inside the Black Box."

At this stage, with the strict controls on commercially harvested bass, recreational fishing accounts for the greatest impact on bass populations, Vic explains. "At the same time that we've seen the commercial fishing industry decrease, we've certainly seen the recreational fishing in this area explode. Years ago you never saw advertisements for striped bass trips on open boats [so-called head boats with dozens of anglers]. A few charter boats [up to six anglers] ran striped bass charters in the fall, mostly around the moons. There wasn't anything like the activity we see these days. Charters are now doing two to three trips a day. Open boats like the *Viking* and the *Marlin* are doing striped bass trips. The pressure that is being applied to the bass by sportfishermen is selective pressure: they all keep the biggest fish. The result is, we have lots of fish but you don't have quality in the fishery, meaning quality in terms of size and weight, the chance at least that you can catch a forty- or fifty-pounder. Those odds have been diminishing quickly over the last ten years.

"I've seen the results in the changes in the size distribution of the fish that I sample every fall. I'm catching thousands of two-, three-, four-, five-year-old fish. Before '95 I used to catch fish up to fourteen to fifteen years old. And, way back ten to twelve years ago, forty- and fifty-pounders, with some degree of regularity throughout the fall. I haven't seen a fifty-pound fish since 1994."

I offer a comparison. "Is it like deer hunters targeting all the trophy bucks until you are just left with the small deer with unimpressive antlers?"

"Not entirely, I don't think that the big fish are all gone. They're around but they're not inshore. They're further offshore or out of reach. The smaller schoolies are more prevalent this time of year. I don't think, and this is my gut feeling, I don't think the bigger fish—and I mean the real big fish, the forties and up—behave the same way. They don't have the same metabolic needs. They can just lay where they are and feed at will and they don't have to be as aggressive and proactive in terms of the way that they school or move around. They have a little bit more selectivity and they can tolerate more temperature extremes."

I tell Vic that my friends in the flyfishing business are doctrinaire catch-and-release anglers. This, no doubt, is a holdover from troutfishing practice in which Americans are the leading conservationists. A trout in a stream is usually at or near the top of the food chain. Top predators are always few in number—there are always more zebras than lions, more chickens than chicken hawks. Bass, though they are predators, are not top predators. There are many animals that can eat them, sharks for instance. They often travel in herds of thousands of fish. They are by nature abundant, in part because their prey is so numerous. Still, the flyfishermen hold that recreational fishermen account for the greater part of a bass harvest that is threatening the species. Two fish per day (which is the state limit on charter boats) is unconscionable to their way of looking at things. "You don't burn your golfballs," Paul often remarks to explain why we throw fish back.

This catch and release stand has greatly exacerbated relations between the flyrod guides and the old-time charter captains. They feel that the position of the flyrod guides, expressed by their newly formed association (Ernie French, an ardent conservationist, being one of the founders), is potentially damaging to their business. When someone came down to Ernie's slip this summer and reversed the bilge pumps on his SeaCraft, thereby sinking it, some felt it was a disgruntled member or associate of the old-time captains who was at fault. Others pointed to an altercation on the water with another flyrod guide who Ernie had upbraided for crowding him. Case unsolved, but the fact remains that fishing guides are a disputative, quick-to-anger breed, and any change in fishing regulations is sure to upset someone, if not everyone.

I return us to the question of size and angling. "What anglers are looking for is more big fish, Vic. I know I was happy as could be with the old thirty-six-inch limit we had ten years ago."

"You're not alone," he agrees. "What we are hearing from

the recreational industry is that they want to see more quality in the fishing experience. By more quality, they mean a reasonable chance of catching a large fish—thirty-, forty-, fifty-pound fish. That goal is possible but it takes time. You have to give the fish time to grow and it takes a long time to grow fish thirty to fifty pounds, and you have to protect fish from harvest when they are small if you want to grow them large. When we closed the fishery in '84 through '85, ostensibly because of PCBs, it took until 1995 until the stock was back and there were large fish."

"Where do our stripers come from, Vic? I remember fifteen years ago, I wrote a story for *Field & Stream* about the Point, and I spoke with Steve Sautner at the Littoral Society [a coastal conservation group]. He sent me some papers on bass and blues. I was surprised at how little we understood the comings and goings of these fish. Basically what those papers said is south shore fish on Long Island come from the Chesapeake, while Long Island Sound fish come from the Hudson, and the two stocks rarely, if ever, mix."

Now I am on Vic's scientific turf and he disagrees quite animatedly. "How can anybody know that? How can anybody formulate an opinion? That's just absurd to begin with.

"Bass are coastal fish. The historical records show that two hundred years ago, they were in every stream on the coast. They were so thick that farmers used striped bass for fertilizer. What we have and have always had is a mixed coastal stock. True, the Sound is a nursery area for Hudson River fish, but it also contains mixed coastal fish from the Delaware and the Chesapeake. We tag fish and there's ten to fifteen other people like me, up and down the coast, tagging striped bass for scientific study. One of the things we do every year, twice a year, is get together and look at our tag returns. Guys in the Chesapeake, guys in the Hudson, guys like myself, guys on the Cape, guys on the Outer Banks. We see the movement and the migration of fish and the thing is, with few exceptions, all the fish move. Everybody gets the same result. North up to Massachusetts in June and July, then in September, October, November south again, past Montauk Point in the fall. One thing I have found is that our fish are generally native to a region that stretches from the Gulf of Maine down to a few degrees south of New Jersey."

"And what about the Autumn Run, Vic? Paul Dixon says it starts when the big fish congregate and key in on the bait on the south side of the Point. As the season goes along, schools of smaller fish, all in year classes, join them. The number of bass gets larger and larger until, if it is a good year, there will be a blitz from Montauk Village all the way around the Point to Montauk Harbor. Do you agree?"

"Yes."

"Will this be a strong run?"

"Right now, you know more than I do. I need the seas to calm down and for us to get our net in the water. Ask me in a week. Every year is different. My gut is, this is turning out to be a good year."

Shortly after Vic leaves, Paul calls. He and Amanda stayed on the Point until nightfall. True to the current script, the bass came up. "The tide was brown with bait and the bass were raging," Paul says. "Thirty-four, thirty-five inches, mongo fish."

I call Jim Clark and tell him the score. If you want big fish, you have to get your boat in there and flash some elbows with the rest of the fishermen. That's how Montauk works. There are rhapsodic moments of flyfishing bliss to this, but this is not the pure, contemplative Zen fishing that being alone on a remote trout pool offers.

"I'm fishing with Jim Levison tomorrow. You're coming, he drives, we fish. Deal?"

"Deal," Jim says.

# October 5: Blitz

≋

THE TWO JIMS, Levison and Clark, meet me at my house at ten in the morning. Levison is an ex-New York City cop whose fifteen minutes of fame was as the lead detective in the Bernie Goetz case. Skinny as angel hair pasta, bald and bespectacled, he looks like neither the classic NYPD flatfoot nor the idealized flyrod guide. After twenty years on the force, first walking the beat, then as a detective, he has seen the absolute worst and darkest of humanity. Flyfishing isn't the only thing in the world that is the polar opposite of murdered prostitutes and torched homeless people, but it is the thing that Jim has found. He stopped chasing murderers and started chasing fish. He is extremely chatty. Maybe that's why he was a good detective: He got people to talk because he made them crazy to get a word in edgewise.

Jim drives a huge Ford van with 150,000 miles on it. It is very much a fishingmobile. It is loaded with flyrods, fly boxes, back issues of fishing magazines, rain gear, cold weather gear and a comfy bunch of old towels and sweaters that make a fine travelling bed for his dog Jake, an agreeable Labrador.

Levison's boat is a Parker, a sleek center console that he keeps luminously white. His equipment is pretty: Reddington rods, hot with the guides this year, Able reels, likewise the expensive high-tech reel of the year, sinking head lines, orange running line.

We head straight into an east wind, a brisk 15 knots. There is an old fishing saying, *wind out of the east fish bite the least.* Not true. East can be uncomfortable but the fishing can be fine. As we reach the Point, Amanda and Bob Sullivan are fishing the north side on a little outcropping they call the False Point, a few hundred yards west of the true point. There's a boulder there, which at most times is submerged. Right up against it, the fish boil like crazy. Tommy Cornicelli, a flyrod guide from Moriches, is among them. Cornicelli, a tough Italian American from Brooklyn, has the same don't-screw-around-with-me demeanor as the gonzo wetsuit guys. In the late fall he runs duck and goose shoots. He thrives on bad weather. A day like this turns him on.

The bass are in a tight formation and furious in their pursuit of bait, but we leave that pod to the boats that are already there. Cornicelli rides alongside us to the south side. Paul rounds the Point, returning from a morning charter. He waves us off with a big theatrical gesture.

"Go back, go back, no fish here," which means, of course, that the fishing is exploding.

We stop for a gam.

"I have never seen them so tight to the rocks," he adds. "You can roll cast from the beach and catch them. At 'em boys!"

Jim waves, grins and pushes the throttle down full. We pause below the radar tower at Camp Hero, the old army installation that got its name because the returning soldiers from the Spanish-American war, heroes of the Battle of San Juan Hill, were decommissioned there in 1899. When I first fished here in the mid-1980s, the radar tower had a forbidding Dr. Strangelove feel. Now, fallen into desuetude, it is a kitschy Cold War knickknack on the breakfront of the American shore.

We see bass in the wash of the breakers, close to the beach. A guy in a floppy hat trundles behind the fiercesome wetsuit quartet who have taken up their positions atop their usual rocks. The floppy hat guy carries two big bass. He waddles down the shore holding up the fish by the jaw, and somehow he manages to hold a rod in one hand as well. A boy walks alongside him with another trophy fish. His face beams with the beacon smile that all boys who have had great fishing success wear.

The swells are big, not the biggest we have seen, but the combination of southwest swells and a strong east wind makes for a confused ocean. Where normally you can time the swells and back in to get a cast off close to shore, today there's nothing to do but wait. The breakers collapse on the shore with the dull report of distant artillery. Then bait darkens the water. Following that by no more than a few seconds the bass rampage begins. I look and see that there are bass to the east all the way to Montauk Point and likewise to the west around Caswell's Point: two miles of herding, eating and killing.

A school of bass comes straight to our boat. I connect six times but cannot set the hook. I think it is because there is no lead weight on the head of my fly so it doesn't drop in front of their eyes. The bass swim under us. They are not bothered by, and take no notice of, our presence.

Whatever it is that has been happening at Montauk just changed today. It's growing more intense. The black and silver bass, the free-form brown swatches of penned-up bait, the streaks of white foam where bait and prey join combat, all look like a living Jackson Pollock canvas—abstract and chaotic. We have to shout in order to hear one another over the marauding fish.

A red speedboat—a seaborne version of a Hell's Angels Harley—cuts between us and the shore. The bass-crazed driver rams into the pod. He casts and hooks a fish. So does his sidekick. They horse the fish into the boat and take two more. I don't know who is more blinded with blood lust, the anglers or the fish.

A flycaster stands on the shore. He is at the apex of the semi-circular cove. The bass throw up foam all around him. He seems to be standing on bass. Maddeningly, we are too close to shore so we must hold our fire.

"Think about it," says Levison. "We live in the Metropolitan area. If you run a circle fifty miles around Manhattan, there are probably twenty million people. There are a few hundred thousand fishermen among them, men and women who love to fish, and we are in one of the best blitzes that Montauk has seen in years, yet there are three boats working. Maybe there's a hundred surfcasters on the shore. We have an incredible natural phenomenon virtually to ourselves. Tens of thousands of anglers around the world would have paid me any price I asked to have seen this and here we are ten lucky schmucks in the mega blitz."

We look back toward the Point. Against the cloudy, steamy and dark sky, the lighthouse stands on the bluff like a tall white candle. We move east, following the falling tide. The bass have the bait backed up against the rip.

Instantly, Clark hits upon the right motion for today's fishing in the rocking and rolling sea. He starts stripping as the fly hits the water. This keeps his fly line tight, with no slack, so that when a bass strikes he can strike back. He catches three bass within ten minutes, all of them healthy. He keeps one for the family.

A lone monarch butterfly beats its way into the wind. Oddly, there are no ducks and geese on the wing. I haven't seen them for three days. Not many gulls and terns, for that matter, even though the bass, blues and albacore have rounded up easy pickings for them.

Jim Levison spins the wheel. We head back into the waves to make another run over the pod of fish under the lighthouse. Clark and I each hook one quickly. When I lean over to get mine, I wrap the leader around my hand in order give me a better purchase on the hook. A wave comes at us broadside. Jim turns the boat to avoid taking its full force. The boat pitches and I feel the whole weight of the bass pulling on the line around my hand. It shakes its body; I watch its muscles ripple as it tears the line from me. It leaves me with a freely bleeding cut on my finger where the line ripped across it. I pump the fish in again and grab the bass by the lower lip, a maneuver that will temporarily immobilize many fish long enough to extricate the hook. We weigh it, eleven pounds.

"This one is for my family," I say as I toss it in the live well.

I try another cast. A bass hits with great force, more than I have ever felt. This can be deceiving in moving water. Even a small fish that turns its side to the current will feel bigger and stronger. After one lunge to the left and another to the right I can tell from the shakes of his head that he is big and strong. He dives, straight down to the rocks on the bottom. I pull back as hard as I can. My tackle is heavy-duty—it can take all the pressure I can give it, so I lean into the fish. But he will not move.

Levison tries to hold steady in the pounding seas. He times each surge of power to the engine according to the waves. I pull back hard. The bass shakes its head, not wildly but quickly as if to rid itself of an annoyance. I don't know how long this goes on. Subjectively, a half hour. In reality, maybe six minutes. Finally the leader parts, perhaps from the bass rubbing against the rocks. The rod springs back. I nearly fall over backward.

"Big one," Levison says sorrowfully.

"Jesus, I thought I could turn him," I lament. "Jim, I'll drive, and you fish now. They're still all around us."

I take the wheel to let Levison have his innings. I try to combine the three maneuvers of avoiding the rocks, facing into the waves that come at us from more than one direction and putting Levison on fish. A pod surfaces. He gets his fly into it and strikes hard at a good fish.

"There, you s.o.b," he tells the bass as if to send a message to the one that I lost.

Jim runs aft to clear the prop before the fish wraps him. He holds the rod over the gunwales so that the fish will swing wide, but it decides to go right under us. His rod bends. The line wraps the prop. He reaches and tries to free it. While the seas, which have grown nastier, pound us, I hold Jim's belt loops as he leans over and, failing to extricate his line, cuts it. I turn the wheel hard left and gun the engine away from the rocks.

I have never had to cut the line around a prop, and now it has happened twice in two days. We take it as a sign and decide to call it a day. The tide pours out of the bay, meeting the swells and the wind head on. We climb the waves and slide down them the whole way back, happy, finally, to come into the sheltering arms of the harbor entrance.

We are all very pleased. It looked like a nothing day when we started, but we had the good fortune to come upon a blitz that was so little pressured that it felt like it was us and all the bass in creation, nothing else.

On the drive back to my house, Jim makes phone call after phone call. This is standard guide practice: fish all day, make calls from the car and hope there is enough time for a shower, dinner, and everything that has stacked up on the answering machine. Feed the dog, too. There usually isn't a wife or girlfriend at home to do that. Very few guides get married, fewer stay married or even stay in a relationship. Fish, phone, food, sleep. Not much time for a relationship.

When we arrive home, Jim Clark takes his fish and thanks us for the day. I am enormously pleased to have put him into a Montauk blitz. I fry up some bluefish for Levison and myself, with crisped capers, lemon juice, olives and tomatoes. I dice three potatoes and crisp them in melted duck fat with lots of black pepper. The fresh fish, the crispy potatoes, the tangy vegetables and a bottle of wine maintain our splendid mood. The autumn blitzes have arrived.

That night, I dream:

*I am in a ballroom in Havana where I once made a film about Ernest Hemingway. Papa sits in a chair with a broomstick, pushed through the handle of a bucket filled with water. He lifts the bucket with the broom handle. "I do this for three weeks.*

*Gets me in shape for marlin," he says. He asks me to try, but I can't. My hand hurts like hell, the cut where the bass broke me off.*

I wake from my dream. The hand hurts. I walk onto the deck outside my bedroom door. The air is cool and damp but not unpleasant. Tomorrow, everyone will be at the Point. "Word will be out," Levison predicted when he left.

# Friday, October 6:
# Stripers in the Mist

≈

PAUL PHONES AT 6:30. Amanda calls at 6:33. They are jazzed about yesterday's blitz. Am I coming out on the water today?

"They said west winds, twenty knots. You can't get to the south side," I mumble.

"It's flat calm at the mouth of the harbor," Paul counters.

But I am dead to the world. Usually a great day of fishing, like yesterday's, and the prospect of another to follow will have me wide awake before dawn. But I am yet not used to fishing all day, every day. I am tired—muscles, bones, head, all of me. I look out the window. The bay is covered with fog and a light rain falls. I cannot see Gardiners Island. I close my eyes.

Jim Levison calls at 10:00.

"I figured we'd stay out late, so why get up early. Should we do it?"

"My house, a half hour?"

Jim pulls up at 11:30. We stop at The Springs store. Two women in front of us go over a big order. Cold cut platters, hors d'oeuvres, cheeses, salads.

"Big feast, an occasion?" I ask.

"A big one."

"Birthday?"

"No, we're getting married," the two ladies answer.

When they leave, Andrea, the Ecuadoran woman who works behind the counter, joins me in a wondering laugh at our modern times. We get to gabbing in Spanish. I ask her what smells so good.

"Arroz con pollo (chicken with rice). I make it every Friday." She offers me a taste. Saffron rice, chunks of chicken, bell peppers, onions, peas. We forget about sandwiches.

The fog is thick as we drive the Napeague flats. I hope it is not so bad at the Point, but fear, if anything, it will be even thicker. Still, we know for sure that the bass and the bait will return because nothing has happened to upset their pattern.

We take East Lake Drive to Gin Beach, where we can check the fog and the seas from the breakwater at the mouth of the harbor. The sea is calm, the fog is lifting. There is a misting rain, but it is soft and, if not warm, then at least not cold. An overcast like the one we have now *always* helps the fishing. Jim and I race to his boat, tear out of the harbor and make for the Point. The prospect of good angling pulls us as if we were hounds on a leash.

There are a half dozen surfcasters on the north side, but there are no boats on the rip under the lighthouse. Paul and Amanda are not in sight nor do they answer their phones. It all can mean only one thing—south side, big time.

Sure enough when we round the Point the surfcasters are spaced out like a line of police along a semi-crowded parade route. The bass feed on the surface, the surf guys sling their lures, fight fish, land fish. The whole flyfishing fleet is there plus a few new faces—outsiders. You can tell these last because they run almost across the lines of the real Montaukers, almost founder on the rocks, almost get hit by the surfcasters' plugs, almost collide with other boats. Like an extremely near-sighted person, excusing his way through a crowd, they stop, start, hesitate, lunge.

"Well there's fish here, for sure," Jim says, "but if it's like yesterday, there are fish west of us as well and maybe not so many people. Let's run west and look."

"Hit it, captain."

We head to the first break in the bluffs, the Sewer Pipe, not a particularly lyric name for a fishing spot, but an accurate one. It is the old outflow from Camp Hero. The sewage is gone along with the soldiers, but the pipe is still there as a landmark. In the calm seas, directly in front of it, the bass are plainly visible—a bubbling black disturbance on the gray-green water. On the shore, the surf breaks in gentle rollers, a fringe of white that the surfcasters can easily reach. The plugs of the surfcasters land in front of us. I caution Jim, "I think you are getting a little close to the surf guys."

"Hey man," he says with a touch of the old cop in him, "they think they own the first hundred yards of water. The fish are here so we're here."

This line of reasoning is not going to add to comity between the flyfishing and surfcasting tribes. On the other hand, there are fish right in front of us and we are fishermen, so we fish for them.

The plugs and heavy metal lures of the surfcasters come straight at us. I can watch the whole line streaking toward me. It looks like they are firing at us because the bass are directly in front of us. The lures land, the lines go instantly taut as one surprised, enraged bass after another is pulled from the pack. Gleeful imprecations rise in chorus from the shore.

Jim and I cast into the swarming bass. I come tight against something. I pull, it pulls. It is not a fish. I am tangled up with one of the surfcasters, make that two, make that three. If we are not careful we will have the whole phalanx on the shore—ten or twenty anglers—with crossed lines. I expect a fusillade of curses. But when I say, "Let me pull the lures in. I can get to them in the boat," everyone is calm.

"Okay," they shout.

"Let out more line," I request.

They do. I have us unhooked in five minutes. "Sorry," I offer. But there are so many fish busting no one takes much notice. Had I executed this tangling maneuver when fishing wasn't so good, I would have had a surfcasting lynch mob on my hands, bent on killing me with shrapnel made of fish hooks and lead weights. But good fishing often makes for lower tempers. Not always. Often.

"Let's get out of here, Jim." I don't want to press my luck.

We end up at Caswell's. For some reason it is a spot the stripers favor and it fits my fishing style. All flyfishing—make that all fishing—has its lucky places. There are always charmed spots on a trout stream; when a particular mayfly hatches on a river, the bugs may be in the air everywhere, but there will be pools and eddies that are the right place to be because the fish concentrate there and, more to the point, they are catchable. It has to do with currents, depth, and things as personal as your casting style. One kind of bend in a river or lee on the shore will favor a righty, others a lefty, and so on. Caswell's is my tailor-made spot.

Yesterday's Visigoths in the red boat are back for more high-speed carnage. While they roar back and forth, we wait.

If you have good eyes, you can read the deep signs that the

water always displays. You will see things before the other boats and surfcasters do. When that happens, Paul Dixon has told me, never point . . . *never*. Don't shout. Look as if there is no sign of fish anywhere. And slowly, as if you are cluelessly searching, idle over to where the fish are about to explode.

When I began fishing this fall, I would not have understood this advice, because the signs Paul talks about, the same ones Jim or any guide looks for, were invisible to me. All I could see was the climax of the process where bait being herded ended in a feeding frenzy. It was not until the fish busted on the surface that I would get excited and jump up and down and yell "Over there! Fish!"

My guides always see the signs way before the fish come to the surface. Seeing fish or signs of fish, like everything else in successful angling, requires time on the water. If I go bone fishing, I get out on the flats that first day and when the guide says, "Fish at ten o'clock, forty feet," I see nothing. After two or three days on the water, though, I see the forked tail tips of the bonefish as if there were a a neon sign above them.

Likewise with spinners on trout streams. The spinner is the last stage of the mayfly's life. It has clear wings and an elongated tail—beautifully elegant. Right after copulation for the first, and last, time in its life cycle, the female lays her eggs and expires on the surface of the stream next to her fallen mate. I never used flies that imitated spinners for my first twenty years of flyfishing. People I respected always advised me to try, but I had no idea what the rise of a trout to a spinner looked like. Then, one afternoon on the Delaware River, Al Caucci, a pioneer of modern dry flyfishing, stood next to me and said, "There. There. Over there. That one. There!" He kept pointing out the subtle rise of a trout to a spinner until I learned to discern the tiniest dimple in the surface of the moving stream. Once I recognized one rise, the pool was alive with dimpling trout. Since that time, I fish spinners as much as I fish normal dry flies.

So it is with learning to see signs of bait and stripers. The bait fish are the saltwater version of the mayfly: the plentiful food that the gamefish key in on. After days of staring at the water, in full sun and twilight, in wind, fog and rain, today I can finally see it all happening. First there is a darkening, a shadow in the water, deep down. The shadow spreads like a wine stain on a white tablecloth. It comes nearer to the surface. The sea birds, always on the lookout for easy food, may start to assemble and circle over the shadow that takes on color as the gamefish push the bait toward the surface. The stain is now a swatch of color—brown with orange and red. Next, the baitfish leap from the water into the air as they flee the predators. Finally, all you see is fish and foam and noise and birds—a free-for-all.

Jim and I wait. There is nervous water all around. There are bass among the rocks, but we cannot risk our boat there. A huge school forms in front of them. The fish come up eating and slashing: They sound like hand-pushed lawnmowers. We make our move.

*Approach.*

*Keep your rod low.*

*Hold your breath.*

*Ease up on them.*

*Cut your engines.*

We back in, let go a cast, hook up, and move out to avoid the rocks. I catch a fish, Jim does, too. Then another, and another. A few blues mixed in with the stripers. The school of baitfish feints and parries, moving fifty feet at a time to escape the stripers. But the bass are like border collies herding lambs. Too fast, too quick. We catch a dozen fish, keep one. Not bad for such a late start.

When the fishing slows, we dig into our arroz con pollo. Jim, a fine photographer, shoots pictures of the gray, slightly misted shore and the ghostly shapes of surfcasters.

My Hemingway dream of last night is still with me and brings back a story that I think Jim will like. In 1983, I fished for three weeks with Papa's old boat captain, Gregorio Fuentes. He was 86 then, he is 101 now. I used to smuggle five cigars and a flask of rum onto our boat every day (which his doctors advised him against consuming for health reasons). I believe he has outlived all of his physicians. One day, when we were drifting off Moro Castle waiting for a sign of fish, the same way we drift off Montauk waiting for our quarry, Gregorio told me a story. That's what you do to pass the time on a fishing boat. Stories about other places and fish most of the time.

"When the most successful madame in Havana died," Gregorio said, "Papa and one of the Du Pont heirs paid for her funeral. It was a big procession with a band through downtown Havana. Papa told the members of the Cuban Senate, who were all regulars at the *casa de putas*, that they had to march behind the old whore's casket. If they didn't Papa would never invite them to another party. So they all marched to bury the old lady and their wives saw their pictures on the front page of the paper."

"Should have happened to our Senate," Jim says. "Probably could have."

The fishing never starts up again so we return to Diamond Cove Marina, where Jim moors his boat. It is an idyllic little haven. A Mexican woman, Frida, presides from her post in the office, watching CNN, selling bait, gear, candies and soda. She is in radio contact with most of the fishing boats between Montauk and Cape Cod. Everyone who fishes stops in to say hi and bye. No one has a more comprehensive picture of Montauk angling every day than Frida.

The marina owner is Skip, a man with an All-American, Jimmy Stewart smile. Skip spends the day directing the comings and goings of boats, the repairs, the selling of fuel. He also smokes bluefish and gives me two. I will serve them warm with raw onion rings and a slice of lemon.

Diamond Cove feels like a small town at the end of the day. The people who overnight on their boats make dinner, watch the news, clean their gear. As we walk down the dock two guys from New Hampshire, completely in the dark about the flyfishing here, ask Jim what kind of flies are good for albies. Jim gives them a handful of the epoxy flies that we use.

A large woman with a Chockaloskee, Florida, T-shirt relaxes with a generous cocktail on the deck of her cabin cruiser. It is paneled in dark wood. She has the weather radio on, so I recognize the Robot's voice. Her husband surfaces from the cabin. He is tanner than shoe leather. He cradles a white miniature bulldog.

"Fishin' good, boys?"

I tell him it has never been better and he gives us a big thumbs-up then wiggles the dog's paws for emphasis.

We head to my place, where Paul joins us for dinner. Amanda and her friend Rhett—as in drinking buddy but not necessarily boyfriend—show up at the last minute. Amanda doesn't have a boyfriend, she has some guys she sees. She reminds me very much of Nola Darling, the main character in a movie by Spike Lee, *She's Gotta Have It*. It is an arch comedy of manners set among African Americans in Brooklyn that hinges on one delicious conceit. What if a woman acted like a man? In this case, Nola is pursued by three men, all deeply in love with her. They all want a commitment. Usually in life, it's the woman who wants to do the nesting and the guy wants to gad about. Not here. Nola is independent and the guys are the gushy romantics.

Amanda has a trail of men in love, in like, in deep interest. The last thing on her mind is getting serious. She is definitely not looking for Mr. Right, but she seems quite content with a few Mssrs. Right Now. I don't know, don't ask, the details of any of these relationships. I just know Amanda, in her breezy way, has drinking buddies, fishing buddies and maybe a boyfriend buddy or two. Rhett fits somewhere in this spectrum.

While we polish off two bottles of wine, I pan roast the bass on Pierre's stove-top skillet, a piece of black iron about one and a half inches thick. It gets very hot and the heat is even all over. The thick bass fillet cooks in five minutes. I serve it with a sauce from one of the recipes that I learned from Gray Kunz last year: tarragon, green peppercorns, honey, lemon juice and salt. The combination produces the desired effect on the diners. All the fish and all the sauce disappear.

Over dinner I mention that I went to Caswell's to miss the crowd and ask Paul why we didn't see him there.

"That's because we had huge bass nearer the Point—every one thirty-four inches plus."

My fishing with Jim had been superb, but no giant fish like Paul was catching.

"Well we were all on the Point for a while, what did you see that we didn't?"

"There were huge schools of albacore so we drifted into them. I told my clients that we were going to take two or three of them and when we did, we would draw a crowd. Sure enough we hook one albacore, then another, then there are half a dozen boats on this huge pod. I tell my guys, 'We can stay here and play with the albacore, but the bass were here, the tide is moving and then the bass will move with the tide. If we sneak out of the pack now and find the bass, the boats are going to stay on the albacore and we will have the bass to ourselves . . . okay?'

"They are fine with that so we move to the western end of Turtle Cove. We see a huge brown mass. I tell them it's going to happen any minute and then it busts loose—the bait are up, then the bass are up. We are the only ones fishing them. The rest of the fleet is still on the Point doing the albie shuffle. I haven't seen mongo fishing like this in a long time."

Confirming, in laymen's terms, what Vic Vecchio has expressed more scientifically, he adds, "The fish always gather in groups—today it was the albies on the point, the smaller bass on the north side, and the mongos where we were. Some thirty-pound fish! It is a massive force of nature. And we're just getting started. Pray for weather, Peter."

## October 7:
## Witching Water

≈

THE SUN LEAPS OVER Gardiners Island. Nothing but blue in the sky. A northwest wind brings in air as clear as a windowpane and, with it, long flights of geese, the first I have seen in four or five days. They extend from one end of Gardiners, past Cartwright's shoal at the other end and on to Montauk.

Melinda and my youngest daughter, Lily, are due on the train in early afternoon. Josh and I will fish the morning with Bob Sullivan, who has started to guide for Paul this season. Bob's main business is the manufacture of a line of fishing hats, tote bags and T-shirts called Dizzy Fish. They all feature a logo of a fish skeleton with a star and spiral emanating from the skull—the standard comic strip representation of a knock on the head.

We leave the harbor with the west wind behind us. The tide comes in from the east. *Why is it always wind against tide?* I ask myself. But the answer would be the same as it is to the question, "Why does the wind always blow in your face when you have to get off a quick cast." I suppose nature's answer would be, "Don't complain, at least you are fishing."

It's a rough, slow ride. The waves come at us. The spray clobbers Josh. I am likewise rinsed but I am wearing my skins—

the local term for waterproof clothing. From time to time we rise over a wave. The prop comes out of the water momentarily. It coughs fumes that blow back at us. Then the prop churns the water again. We crawl through the rip at Shagwong and on to the Point where the waters are even angrier.

It is hard to make out the bait wads in the chop, but there is some activity close to shore. Too close for us. There are albacore in the rip, but they are scattered and the water is unfishable, at least not comfortably fishable, in Bob's flats skiff.

Once around the corner and on the south side, the waves come at our stern as we now move into the wind. Not as wet, though no bargain. We move on to Caswell's. Because it juts out from the southern shore, if we creep into the deepest part of its curve, we are protected from the wind. We can drift almost to the shore. At the western edge of the cove the underwater boulders always hold bass.

No more than five feet from shore I look into the green swirling water. The sunlight comes from the east at this hour and just over my shoulder. Bob silences the engines and we drift with the tide. A school of rainbait, perhaps six feet below us, turns and catches the morning light on each tiny fish's silver side. The shafts of light, the shimmering shifting shape of the bait school, the jade green water, the swollen forms of the undersea boulders—the living mass of twinkling rainbait looks like a stained-glass window. At one moment all you see is pattern, then a melting of color and shape into pure mood. It is water that speaks to you as a dream does—you can almost hear it, almost understand, but you never succeed in fully grasping what you think it is telling you. Maybe it is saying that this is what the earth feels like when it's alive.

There are four places where I have seen this kind of water,

I call it Witching Water. The first is where the Lackawaxen flows into the Delaware River, where Zane Grey lived for twelve years. The main stem of the river curves away from the inflow of the Lackawaxen. The waters of the confluence are green and clear and rocky. In the spring, when the dogwood is in bloom, there are always a few john boats anchored there fishing for the fishing schools of shad that pause in the eddies of the merging streams.

The second place is at the Boca of the Chimehuín in Argentina. The Chimehuín is unusual in that it flows out of a lake rather than into one. Lake Huechulaufquen, I believe, fills the caldera of an ancient volcano. A crack in its rim creates an opening through which the waters of the Chimehuín begin their flow to the pampas. The water rushes, swirling and green, in the cold days of March when the brown trout leave the lake and run downstream to spawn. Bebe Anchorena, an Argentine gallant of surpassing style, caught both the world record dry fly *and* wet fly brown trout in that stretch of river. I fished there in a cold driving rain and watched the current curl around the deep rocks. There was an alive shape, like a fat green snake in each tendril of current, like Ophelia's flowing hair in the stream where she drowned herself—"a creature, native and indued unto that element."

East of Key Largo a wide coral flat ends in a channel about one hundred yards from shore. When the tarpon don't show in other places, the seasoned guides know that there is always a resident platoon of them here. The waving turtle grass ends at a patch of white sand where the water deepens. The tide flowing off the flat and sweeping down the channel is a dependable conduit for bait. The sun lights up the depths and filters through the grass. If you drift over that channel and wait for fifteen minutes, you will always see the tarpon prowling. Their huge silver scales pick up the sunlight in the green tropical water. Similarly, when striped pass under our boat in Montauk—in groups of a hundred, sometimes a thousand—their sides reflect the same hues.

All of these places and their emerald shimmering waters never fail to tap a deep feeling. It is at the core of my love of angling. It is a feeling of transcendence. The fish cannot hear me, three meters underneath the surface, but, still, when I see them going about life, unmindful of my gaze, I hold still as I would if I had come upon a mermaid combing her hair in the reflection of a tidal pool. I don't want to speak to her, or hold her, or touch her. Seeing and not being seen is enough.

Witching Water: on the Delaware, the Chimehuín, in Key Largo, but most of all at Montauk. Montauk's rocky sea floor is lined with boulders that ten thousand years of wind and storms have pulled from the sandy cliffs. The ocean bottom here is white and green and just deep enough to bend the light like antique glass and to reveal the shadowy silver shapes of game fish. When the Autumn Run is in full swing, Montauk is a church with stained-glass windows that look down on six miles of ocean, carpeted with fish.

On this morning with Josh and Bob, we gaze at the schools of bait and drift over a wide white patch of sand. Four very large bass cross our path. Then another dozen. We look back to the west and see their dark forms against the sand, like tarpon, like torpedoes in slow motion. I cast a sinking fly ahead of an approaching school. I let it settle to the bottom and pull it toward me in swift jerks, like a baitfish trying to escape. The bass ignore it. I have time to lift my fly and cast across their path, but that is a maneuver that can never work. No creature except man is suicidal: A baitfish never swims across the path of a predator, it swims away, always away.

For whatever reason, these fish are not eating. They are on the bottom, moving. There are days like that when the fish you pray to see are all around you, but they show no interest in feeding. Mating behavior, the urge to migrate, the pull of the moon—anglers have many explanations for why fish don't accept their offerings. On this day the bass do not want ours.

It is midday. No doubt the fish will turn on at some point, but my family—coming out for the weekend—needs to be met at the train station. As we round the Point the albies show in a desultory way. Further west, by the rocks they call Stepping Stones, I see a very large angler standing on a rock fifty yards from shore. The waves come up to his chest. He has waded out at low tide and will remain on his rock until the tide peaks and falls again, in four hours. All I see is head and arms and waving rods. I look more closely. The one large angler is actually three anglers sharing one underwater rock. The small blitz that I saw in front of them turns out to be their three plugs cranking through the water throwing up spray.

We slow our engines to avoid swamping them with our wake. A plug lands ten feet from our boat. As it begins to churn water, a bluefish hits it. If a whoop can be said to have a heavy Brooklyn accent, the cry that goes up from the angler fighting the bluefish is purified essence of Flatbush. One of his comrades hooks up with a bass. Another yelp of triumphant pleasure, then nonstop profanities—three middle-aged guys transformed into city kids who curse a blue streak when they are truly happy.

I rush from the dock to meet Melinda's train. She arrives with Lily and Patsy Taylor, our upstairs neighbor in Brooklyn. Melinda and Lily want to go to Clam Bar, our longtime favorite place in the Hamptons. It looks like a standard post–World War II burgers and shakes stand, although its specialties extend beyond that to local seafood, mostly fried. There is no dining room, just a dozen round tables set around the yard adjoining the kitchen. Among its major virtues is a nonstop music selection of great Rock and Roll, mostly black or at least white with an honest level of funk. While I eat a clam roll and sip a glacial Bass Ale, the jukebox plays "Come Go with Me," "Mr. Lee," "Let the Good Times Roll," "Get a Job" and "Not Fade Away" (the original Buddy Holly version).

Lily eats popcorn shrimp, Melinda and Patsy have lobster rolls. The sun is pleasingly warm. The breeze coming off the ocean over the dunes can't decide if it carries summer or fall with it. "Let's take a walk," I suggest, "I have a secret place where you can see the ocean from a high cliff. It's like Big Sur."

Melinda and Patsy like the sound of Big Sur. Lily doesn't know what it is, but she likes the idea of a cliff. Every kid likes cliffs and caves—exciting things happen there. I like the idea because I can look out and see what is happening with the fishing. I am enjoying my family idyll, but still . . .

We turn down a road near the horse ranch midway between Montauk Village and the Point. Whenever I pass it I think of my brother Bobby when he worked for a big-time fashion photographer twenty-five years ago. They were shooting ads here for expensive rums and top of the line cosmetics and perfumes. *Naturellement* there were always acres of the most beautiful women connected with this line of work. On this particular shoot there were five or six Finnish blondes.

"Ooooo . . . ," they said when they saw the horses (most probably the grandparents of today's horses), "ve vill go rideeng on za beach, nude on the horse, and den ve go home and have boiled new potatoes and herrings. Everyone must drink himself one whole bottle of vodka too!"

Neither before, nor since, have I ever considered the combination of potatoes and herring as an effective love elixir. But in the context of my brother's story—which may or may not be true or which I may or may not have embroidered over the years—the thought of those words uttered in a feminine Finnish lilt is uniquely lascivious.

Back in the present, we drive through miles of scrub oak. The pavement ends shortly before the highest of the bluffs. I turn down a dirt road, one that you would miss if you did not know it was there. After two hundred yards, the way is barred, literally, by a long metal bar. I pull my Jeep off the road. I think about taking my rod, but only for a second. *You're taking a stroll with your family.*

We walk the remains of a road that once traversed Camp Hero. The bright green of mid-September still dominates the landscape, but many trees and shrubs have already started to turn yellow and crimson. The rose hips are red and round, big as cherry tomatoes. Two monarch butterflies fly in the air twenty feet ahead of us, as if they too are enjoying an amble on this pleasant road. As we near the bluffs, the forest ends in shrubs and wild flowers. A clifftop border of daises, rose hips and purple asters appears to run into the sky.

"Careful," I caution, "it's a straight drop, a hundred feet." Heights make me nervous and small children near heights only ratchet up my anxiety.

The girls are astonished by the view. Though I know it well, I am too. I don't understand the physics or the optics of it, but it feels like you can see a hundred miles: trawlers on the horizon, a platoon of weekend yachtsmen motoring back and forth with no other purpose than to be on the water, sailboats tacking gracefully with a wind just strong enough to fill their sails and show them off at their best, like greyhounds coming around a turn. Closer in, on the rocky point at Caswell's, the flyfishing flotilla rides the swells. Lily sees fish slashing on the surface.

"Albacore," I tell her, "and a few bass."

As each pod of fish breaks the surface, the randomly arranged boats turn and converge on the commotion. The gamefish encircle the bait and the boats follow the gamefish like a pack of hunting dogs. Nobody is hooked up so I am not missing anything. The green witching water moves gently in and out of the cove.

"Listen," Lily says, "it sounds like a big rattle."

"Lily, when the swells from the ocean come into the shore, they pick up the rocks and drag them in and out. You are hearing the rocks rolling over each other. Every time they do that, a few grains come loose. That is the sound of sand being made."

"Let's go down there," she pleads. Melinda and Patsy are happy to stay up top and take in the view. It is a hump to make it down the cliff, but I have done it before so I know the places to hold on to rocks, to change direction, to test your footing. It's not mountaineering but it does require caution plus a willingness to slide on your butt when gravity demands it.

I lead, Lily follows. When we reach the bottom, she is delighted to be at this hard-to-reach spot. Up close the rumble of the pebbles sounds like drums beating a soft but rapid rhythm. We wave to Paul, Amanda, Bob, Josh, Levison, Clark and Blinken in their boats. *Must be nothing happening on the Point if they are all here.*

There are mussels on the rocky beach, pieces of lobster and crab, silver herring and tiny rainbait all stranded above the high-water mark. A flock of gulls takes flight as we walk the shore. We mean them no harm, in fact would much rather they had stayed and sunned themselves, but wild creatures never want to be around man—or his ten-year-old daughter.

"Mom's probably ready to go, Lil. Let's climb back up."

We grab rocks and branches and pull ourselves up. When we stop to rest at a small shelf of earth midway up the cliff, Lily picks a purple aster and puts it in my hat as an ornament. I follow her up, just in case I need to break her fall. From time to time she can't quite lift herself around a rock, so I push her bottom and up she goes.

We walk out through the forest. I pick a beach plum and chew its tangy flesh.

"Ugh, too sour," Lily says.

# October 8:
## Wrecks and Rescues

≋

THE ROBOT PREDICTS temperatures in the mid-fifties with light winds out of the northwest. He gets the temperature part right, but the wind is cranking.

"Sucks out there, really sloppy," Amanda comments when I meet her at the Crabby Cowboy. It's sheltered on the dock. We lie around and wait for Josh. Amanda frets about the colder weather. I sense the onset of guide burnout. Every guide gets it. Too many days in a row, the milk carton from last week in the fridge, the wet laundry in the dryer just when you need it and you forgot to turn the dryer on, the calluses and charley horses, the same old sandwich because you are too tired in the morning to think of anything else, the temperamental bilge pump, the cracked radio antenna, the cranky clients. Poling her boat on the flats in the summer months, spotting the bass, everything quiet and concentrated—that required one kind of mind-set. Amanda loved it. Layering up against the cold and wet and jostling for space at Montauk is different. As the autumn builds, if you are a guide coming off of five straight months of fishing, part of you wants The Run to get bigger and bigger and part of you wants it to be over.

"Is it tough being a woman guide, the only one out here?" I ask. It is a question that pretty much everyone asks Amanda.

"Not especially. At first I thought I would meet a lot of resistance: Guys are pretty macho about their fishing. But what actually happened is they cut me a little slack, probably more than they would a guy. You're not trying to get away with anything, but they treat you a little differently. After the first five minutes on the boat, though, everything is kind of established. Once they see that you know what you're doing and where you're going and that you know how to fish, they don't think of you as a woman or a man, they think of you as a guide. No one tried to explain that to me at the beginning, especially the other guides, except for Paul."

"And the other guides, Amanda? How did they treat you?"

"Okay now, but at first it seemed they didn't want me to do it. I don't know if it was the woman thing or just more guides on the water."

I think it's the latter. "I have never met two guides who have lots of good things to say about one another. Never happened, not once, in the whole world."

"Everybody trashes everybody," she agrees. "I find comedy in that because no matter what you do or say you will always be wrong in somebody's eyes. You can't fight it and you can't go around with a chip on your shoulder, because it's not worth it. If you can step outside of the guide circle and see these little 'women [the male guides],' like yentas, talking about each other, it's funny. They take it so damn seriously and you can't even joke around about it. I don't know, I always smile when I see that going on."

"How about guys coming on to you?" I ask.

"If you don't act available, they get the message. I'm on the poling platform, the captain of the ship, and they are on the deck below me taking orders. Most guys can't throw their egos around in that position so the dynamics of the boat kind of work to keep things cool."

If you were looking for one phrase to describe Amanda, it would be "stay cool."

Josh arrives. Amanda starts the engines and we take off. The wind follows us to the Point straight from the North Pole: *The cold is coming.*

"I'm going to Honduras as soon as I can," Amanda says. "I'm going to make some calls tomorrow."

We fish the Point hard. Nothing shows in the wild chop. We try the suck 'em up technique, but the fish don't fall for it. The Point looks nasty. There is talk among the guides on the radio of a spate of accidents. Right where we are fishing, a series of swells against the tide capsized a boat yesterday. Luckily an expert surfer was on his board and saw it all happen. He paddled over to the angler (the boat was given up for lost), pulled him onto his surfboard and deposited him safely onshore.

Further east, at Ditch Plains (where the Montauk Bluffs end and the white beaches begin), another boat took a wave broadside. It was Jeff Palmer, a flyfisherman who is out every day during The Run. Jeff chased a bass blitz inside the line of breakers and was so caught up in the fishing that he never saw the approach of the wave that swamped him. Again, surfers came to the rescue. They made it to the boat, bailed it out and, somehow, Palmer got himself pointed into the waves and through them. Worst of all, further east still, at Moriches inlet, the swells from hurricane Isaac capsized a small boat whose engine had failed. Three anglers were rescued, one perished. They are still looking for the body.

The sea takes lives every year. Homer places his sirens on the rocks, luring the sailors to their doom. But if you are a fisherman, there are sirens in the sea as well. They are irresistible. You feel you *have* to be out there fishing no matter what the conditions, and sometimes that is a dangerous, even fatal thing to do. It happens to novices. It happens to experts, and it happens so quickly that you never have time to react.

The greatest disaster in the history of American sportfishing happened at Montauk on September 1, 1951, when a charter boat, the *Pelican*, went down in the rip at the Point. Russell Drumm has written about it in *In the Slick of the Cricket*, his book-length profile of Frank Mundus, the original shark hunter of Montauk (Mundus was the inspiration for Robert Shaw's character in *Jaws*). I also have found accounts of the sinking of the *Pelican* on the audiotapes of the old-time charter captains that I was given by Bill Akin.

According to Gus Pitts, who fished the same waters that day, Captain Eddy Carrol of the *Pelican* was happy to have a more than full load, because he was due to be married the next day. The extra money would make up for taking the day off to tie the knot. This was in the years when the *Daily Mirror*, a now-defunct New York City paper, ran a special Montauk train for fisherman. No sooner had they arrived in Montauk than the work-weary, fishing-crazed anglers would stampede toward the waiting fishing boats.

"They'd get off that train and go through the window and they'd just run. If you fell down they'd go right over the top of you, just like cattle," Gus remembers. "They always told you when you left New York, 'Get on the first boat you come to 'cause if you didn't you won't get a space.' On Sundays the draggers [large commercial trawlers] would come over. They didn't have chairs so they used to put fish boxes on the deck and turn them upside down for the customers to sit on. The customer paid two bucks for the boat, two bucks for the train ride and fifty cents for the icing of the fish and all the beer you could drink."

Frank Mundus was on the dock that morning, newly arrived at Montauk with his boat, the *Cricket*. As he told the tale to Drumm, there were 325 anglers on the train. A man on the dock counted heads and when each boat reached its limit, the command was given to let go of the lines. Then the next boat took on its load. Mundus recalled that the *Pelican* was just ahead of the *Cricket*: "I heard Eddy say, no, no, I got enough." But he was hemmed in, people piling on, and somehow, in the rush and crush, the *Pelican* crammed sixty-one people on its forty-one feet. Equally dangerous, one of the *Pelican*'s engines was out.

Meanwhile, Pitts left the dock and headed across the Sound for tuna. "That morning we went to Watch Hill and we were tuna fishing, just one guy and me and it was beautiful. We started to chum and all of a sudden it was black as night, bright black and I said to the guy, 'Something's coming and it's not good. We need to make a choice. We either stay here and fish and go into Watch Hill and stay over or we get out of here and get home.' The guy said that he had to get home, so we dumped all the chum out and started back."

The northwest wind rose, pushing Pitt's boat unusually fast on the homeward trip. "I had a pair of Crowns, big engines. We were *really* going on those seas. It was unbelievable the speed that we were making."

The northwest wind that drove Pitts across the Sound ran straight into the incoming tide at the Point. The sea stood up like a wall. Pitts' brother, who was fishing close to the *Pelican*, picked up the story: "Eddy came around the Point and the splash of the water soaked everyone on one side of the boat. They all moved to the other side. Then the boat took on a riding sea and she started to go over and capsized. We went over to pull people from the water. The six that I saved were under a canvas bag that formed a pocket of air. If people had worn life preservers we could have saved every one of them.

"Eddy Carrol's brother's boat was out that day. He called and told Eddy to stay out. 'After I unload, I'll come out and take half of your load and bring them in.' But Eddy didn't want to wait. He took the chance and dove in. I threw him a life preserver, but he went down. Drowned."

Other fishing boats joined Ralph Pitts in the rescue effort. The *Bingo II* saved twelve anglers. The *Betty Ann* threw a rope to the stricken ship, but it got tangled and almost pulled the would-be rescue ship over. When the day was over, forty-six people had died. Bodies washed ashore for days.

Ralph Pitts went out with the salvage crew that towed the *Pelican* into port the next day. "When we brought the boat in, there were eleven people who drowned inside the cabin. They all were holding on to one another. A father tied his kid to the rail and he was still there tied to the rail when we took the boat in. A trooper went down into the front cabin. He couldn't take what he saw so I went down. One guy was wedged between the two engines in the engine room. We had to chop open the deck to get him out."

Montauk is dangerous. That's why Amanda's caution about when to go and when to call off a trip makes sense to me. On this day, while we recall the *Pelican* and fish a rip not unlike the one she rolled in, Josh, Amanda and I do not touch a fish in three hours. When the wind rises, we decide to leave before wind and tide collide.

Amanda pulls her hat down low on the return ride. The spray soaks her face anyway. The Plexiglas windshield in front of the center console is, likewise, drenched. She has to lean to one side in order to see while she drives. We come down hard every time we crest the waves that quarter in on us.

I am home in time for a Sunday lunch. My teenager, Lucy, is in the yard with her weekend guest, Camila. They hit a volleyball back and forth. Lily begs to be let in with the big girls and, after some coaxing from me, they include her. I fillet the big bass that I caught earlier in the week with the two Jims. Lily and I walk to the sea wall and toss the head and skeleton into the water. The gulls go right for the skin, but leave the rest. Too big a payload for them.

"The crabs will love it," I tell Lily. "Tomorrow it will all be gone."

Josh opens a cold bottle of white wine. Melinda and Patsy read the Sunday *Times*. I cook up the bass. I lay a piece of fennel on the grill and the bass on top of it. When it is done, we serve it topped with diced, crisped Italian salami and our go-to ingredient, Melinda's roast tomatoes.

*Pop, pop, giggle, giggle*—the sound of the girls hitting the volleyball resumes after the five minutes it takes them to eat. Josh holds a Macoun apple and hits it with the flat of a knife. "They're perfect now. They sound like the pop of the volleyball when you smack one."

"I like the way they fracture like flint when you cut them," I add.

Macoun season has come to have a special meaning for me

this year. Trout fishermen talk about how the shad come in when the dogwoods bloom. In Missouri, I have heard it said the smallmouth start in earnest "when the red buds are no bigger than squirrel ears." Striper time, I realize, coincides exactly with the season when Macoun apples are crispest. When you get your first mealy one, that's as good a sign as any that things have probably peaked.

Josh returns home to "watch football," i.e., nap. Lucy and Camila take their bikes down to Accabonac Neck and the rest of us pile into the Jeep for a ride on the shore at Amagansett. Because the beach bends there, it looks south. So there is sunset over the mainland and sunset over the ocean. Behind us, over the bay, the clouds are rippled with black and a red neon fringe. In the gloaming, the wind-whipped whitecaps are now pinkcaps and redcaps. East and slightly north, the moon rises. The striper moon is coming on full.

# October 9:
# Little Justin, Big Fish

≈

WE HAVE A STRONG GALE coming in at twenty-five knots from the northeast. With the temperature in the low forties it feels like February. When we meet Levison at the dock, Josh says, "You would have to be crazy to try getting around the Point in this wind." Given the weather, Jim and I don't argue.

Still, we know there are fish out there. Jim and I drive to the Point. Since my arrival, I had been planning to spend a day with the surfcasters but, as with every other plan I have had for the month—doing some old-time surfcasting or canoeing the fresh-water ponds—I have abandoned them all for the exhilarating tonic of chasing blitzing bass from a boat. Today I will visit the surfcasters.

The gray sky, the gray ocean, the cold wind that blew half the leaves from the trees overnight all contribute to a wintry mood. The crowd at the parking lot at the Point looks like the tailgating die-hards at a Pittsburgh Steelers game on a January afternoon. Motor homes line the perimeter of the parking lot. Butane tanks and gas-fired barbecues sit behind each trailer. Rods are stacked against bumpers. Waders, mittens, sweaters and parkas hang on makeshift drying racks or, if those are lacking, side-view mirrors, windshield wipers and spare tire mounts serve just as well. The air carries the smells of sausages on the grill and campfire coffee seasoned with wafts of cigar smoke— nothing pricey, more like the Garcia Vegas that I remember Harry Epstein smoking as he raked leaves in the New Jersey neighborhood where I grew up. Smoking and raking were, to Harry, as relaxing as fishing is to me.

For the most part, the men in the parking lot stand around their fires. The women stay inside the motor homes, often in the front seat reading a book. Fisherman outside, fishing wife spending the weekend reading in the car—this is a common sight wherever people fish. *What's in it for the woman?* I often wonder. Also, why does the guy want the woman, who he doesn't say two words to all day, waiting for him in the car? Wouldn't that put pressure on him to cut short his fishing so she doesn't get mad?

Jim and I hop the guardrail and walk to the path that leads to Turtle Cove.

Two portly middle-aged guys trundle up the path. Both wear New York Giants stocking caps. There is no need to ask them how the fishing is. One carries a striper that he claims, and I believe, is thirty-eight inches. The other has one that is not much smaller.

"Nice fish, guys," says Jim. "Are they blitzing?"

"They've been in since daybreak. In and out every fifteen minutes."

We continue on the short, winding path. A man carrying a long white rod and wearing a knit hat with a scampering reindeer and snowflake design jostles us as he rushes down the path. His young child decides that what he most wants to do is to stand in one spot sucking on a Donald Duck pacifier. "Just pick him up and carry him, honey," the impatient angler commands his wife. She tries to coax her toddler to follow Dad, but he won't budge.

"Hell with it, see you down there," he says over his shoulder as he trots down.

We reach Turtle Cove, where angling madness reigns. The bass have created their daily Black Hole—a churning dark patch from which nothing small with fins escapes. Every fisherman is drawn to it. The Black Hole moves in, it moves to the Point, it moves west: The crowd follows . . . tripping, stumbling, casting, fighting fish, tangling lines, everyone barking orders, howling and whooping.

Tom Cornicelli's boat sits just off the rip. It figures. Tom has the kamikaze mentality of a wetsuit surfcaster. He regards rough seas as an in-your-face challenge from Nature. I think he's nuts to be out there, but that might be because when I have nightmares, I see big waves in them. For Tommy, that's a wet dream.

In every group of anglers, there is one person who stands out, who almost glows because he or she "gets it"—understands fishing from a highly developed natural instinct. The Enlightened One on this beach is nine-year-old Justin Delgado, all three-feet-six-inches of him. He slings a nine-foot rod with graceful ease. His neoprene waders are what any pro would wear on such a cold day. When he connects with a fish, he pumps it beautifully.

We strike up a conversation with young Justin, his father, Paul, and his uncle, also Paul. The father works for the phone company, the uncle is in the computer business. They live in Queens and often fish on Jamaica Bay.

"Catch anything, Justin?" Jim asks.

"Bunch of shorts," Justin answers, meaning fish under the

twenty-eight-inch limit. I am tickled by the dismissive and assured way he says this, like a sixty-year-old beach jockey.

I wade in next to Justin and cast my flyrod. The Black Hole moves toward us. The fish appear inside the curl of the waves, like a Japanese painting of an angling scene. It will take a long cast to reach the bass and that means a long backcast as well. There are too many people walking behind me. Most of them have never seen a flyrod so it doesn't occur to them to stay out of the path of my backcast. I give it a rest and watch the crowd.

"You used to come here a lot, Pete?" Jim asks.

"Every day. Sometimes twice."

"Do you miss the scene, all this wacko running around, the action?"

"I did love it, but I wouldn't say that I miss it. It's like pizza. When you are hungry, pizza is great. A perfect slice of pizza is a marvel, but it's not cuisine. Flyfishing is cuisine."

We run into Amanda and a former boyfriend, Peter Smith Johansen (also a guide). Amanda is an accomplished amateur photographer. Since she won't take the boat out on a day when a shipwreck seems more likely than a striper on the line, she spends her day off from fishing taking pictures of other people fishing.

"There's this guy down the beach who caught a forty-pound bass. Chinese guy in a red Jeep, Jack Yee, go talk to him."

"Did he keep the fish?" Jim asks. I am sure he did because surfcasters always keep their fish.

"No," Amanda says, "he let it go."

Jack Yee is happy to talk to us. He is a former truck driver for *The New York Times*. He tells us that the surfcasters call him the Mayor. He has gone to jail and to court to open the beaches to four-wheel-drive vehicles. I tell him that I am grateful to him.

I still find it miraculous that the workaday angler can drive along any shore in the Hamptons, where the price of beachfront property has gone from expensive (millions of dollars) to downright silly (tens of millions of dollars).

While we converse, a wetsuit guy comes over and greets Jack. I recognize him as the same hyper angler who I saw walking up from Ditch Plains a few weeks ago. His name is Josh (not my Josh, just somebody named Josh). He is slim, full of nervous energy like a bird—a contentious bird, maybe a blue jay. Jim and I attempt to join in the conversation. At first he barely takes notice of us. Then, when he does, there is hostility in his tone. Jim says that we are flyrodders. He says he used to flyfish and liked it well enough but that most flyrodders are conceited and snobby. He searches for the *mot juste* to describe flyfishermen and settles on "asshole."

Is this a challenge? Are we supposed to defend ourselves? Attack him? Back down?

He isn't talking about us directly, he explains. He is talking about those "other flyfishermen." So, no, it is not a direct challenge. Then it clicks. I think I understand him. This also explains something about Tommy Cornicelli, whose aggression has always puzzled me, because I genuinely like the guy. With people like Josh Wetsuit and Tommy, their instinctive defense is to surround themselves with an aura of anger and aggression. It is a way of saying, "If you can get past this and still like me then I know you're okay and I can drop my defenses and trust you." In other words, he's not looking for a fight, he's looking for someone who doesn't want to fight him. All that attitude is as if to say get past the anger that he sends out like radar, then you are welcome to land.

We pass the provocation test. Jack and Josh Wetsuit start to share their fishing knowledge with us. They say that the blitz will stop at dark. The big fish will stay in the cove, on the bottom. You need bucktail jigs if you are fishing conventional tackle. "You fly guys will need sinking lines," Josh adds. We're friends now.

Darkness comes on. As foretold, the blitz ends. Another wet-suiter joins us at Jack's truck. He is an ex-driver for the *Daily News*. He comes bearing a tale that I get the feeling he has told a dozen times today and honed to salty perfection.

He was fishing the Point yesterday on the north side when the bass came in (the blitz that Josh, Amanda and I missed when we quit early). The wind seized on the cast of a nearby fisherman and drove it into the neck of our storyteller: It was a plug with three nasty hooks. As he told it: "So I had a fucking plug in my neck, and it's fucking hanging out and the fucking guy with a fucking pin hook starts yanking and says, 'I can't push it through.' So he takes these big fucking nail cutters and he is going on the plug in my neck and then he says, 'I can't get it. Do you have a knife?' Mine is sharp so he takes it and cuts a fucking eighth of an inch of flesh out of my fucking neck and pulls the fucking thing out. Boy was I relieved."

Admiringly, Jim says, "You had someone cut a plug out of your neck with a fishing knife and you're out fishing the next day? You're hard core."

As we drive home, Jim raises Cornicelli on his cell phone. Tom gives us an earful. He says he had the best day of the season, natch, and his was the only boat out there. His angler took a twenty-three-pounder. We—every other flyfisherman who chose not to test the waves and wind—are, in Tom's eyes, candy asses, or worse.

"Crazy mother," Jim says when he hangs up.

# October 10: Sea Mother

~

AT 5:15 A.M. I pull into Vic Vecchio's driveway. There is a light on in the house but I wait in my car. Vic has a wife and kids and I'm not sure that they are up at 5:15 in the morning, or if they are they probably are not ready to receive visitors. I have a thermos full of hot coffee. I turn on the classical station and wait.

Vic closes the door to his house, directs me to park my car on the street and we get into his large van. The cargo space is full of high-tech science gear and low-tech buckets, waders, ropes and landing nets.

"The wind shouldn't bother us," he says, "the high dunes will put us in the lee at Napeague. There may still be some hurricane swells, but I wouldn't be surprised if the water is flat calm."

We head across Old Stone Highway. The trees, thanks to the wind, are noticeably more bare of leaves than they were last night. At the main highway we turn right and, a half mile down the road, into the parking lot of Mt. Fuji, a local sushi restaurant favored by guides.

"The guys on the crew live near here and the parking lot is big enough for all of our vehicles."

Soon, Walter Bennett and his son, Wally (same very extended Bennett family as Harvey at the tackle shop), pull up in an old Ford truck. A twenty-two-foot dory of welded, dark blue metal rests on the flat bed of the truck. Its high prow, like all dories, can breast an incoming wave without taking on water.

Vic makes the introductions. Walter is a taciturn old-timer who chain-smokes Chesterfields. Wally looks about my age (north, but not too far north, of fifty) with a stubbly gray beard. They are followed by Jens Lester (same Lesters as Sam's family: Jens even looks a little like Sam). His son Mitchell, a round-faced quick-to-smile guy in his thirties, sits beside him in their truck. The last to arrive is Mickey Miller. The crew has assembled. Walter Bennett's truck has a load of ripe lobster bait. We make sure that the convoy is upwind of him: We drive to Hither Hills, just east of Amagansett.

The dunes in Hither Hills, threatened and increasingly encroached upon by imbecile developers, extend for miles—gorgeous rolling hills covered with shrubs and flowers. Not a grass-covered dell, though. You clearly see the sand in between the bushes. These dunes and the ones across the highway are literally moving waves of sand: The physics of their motion is precisely the same as a wave in water. True, it takes more time for sand to roll in, heave up and move forward, but with the passage of time, the prevailing force of the waves coming from the south pushes the sands north. The dunes across the highway are known as the Walking Dunes because of this wavelike behavior.

The path we follow was originally an oxcart track. That was the only way the netters and whalers could transport their gear and catch in the old days. Quite often, on the white beaches between Montauk Village and East Hampton, a whale would wash up. It was not unknown for a half dozen carcasses to be found on the beach. Whales were considered the common property of the town. Living whales were also a regular inshore happening. When they were spotted, dories no bigger than ours were launched into the waves and the Bennetts, Lesters and Millers of the last century would pursue them with harpoons.

We pass through the last dune and onto the beach. The sky is a silvery white, the ocean a pewter blanket. We follow Jens Lester. To me the ocean is one unreadable surface. To him, it tells, by a myriad of signs, where to put the net. He checks the direction of the swells, the color of the water that indicates sand bars and channels, the firmness of the sand. Like a fishing guide, he knows where the storms have moved the bars this year, where the fish tend to come close to shore and where they are blocked. On a conscious level, he probably doesn't really know what he knows: He's done it his whole life. Reading this stretch of beach is what he and his father, and their fathers have done for two hundred years.

After a mile we stop at a stretch that looks no different than where we first came through the dunes.

"This should be good," Jens says. That's all the explanation he offers.

"Want to take a ride, Pete?" Vic asks.

I climb up over the truck tires, onto the back of the truck and into the dory with Jens and Mitchell.

Jens watches the waves, times them and, when he is satisfied, gives Wally the signal to gun the truck engine and let her fly in reverse. We speed toward the water. Just before the water's edge, Wally jams on the brakes and we go flying off the back of the trailer like a Brahma bull coming out of a rodeo chute. I feel the jolt as we splash land on the water. In the same instant Jens fires up his old 35-horsepower Johnson and we begin paying out net.

Our course describes a semicircle about one third of a mile in circumference (the old-time nets stretched over a mile). The first part to go out of our boat is the inshore wing. Lead weights on the bottom and floats on the top make an effective escape barrier to any fish inside the net. At the apex of the semicircle there is a large net bag and, continuing back toward shore, another wing.

During the five minutes or so that we let out the net, Walter and Mickey's truck drives down the beach, paralleling us. We head into the beach. Jens times the waves again so that we get the gentlest, least dangerous ride up to the sand. This is a critical maneuver, especially in heavier seas. Trying to come in on the wrong wave will stand the boat on end and pitch its occupants into the water. As with everything else on the ocean, a careless moment or a bad assessment of the waves has led to fatalities.

When we hit the beach, we jump out of the boat. We drag the heavy dory onto the sand, coordinating our heaves with the incoming waves so that we are not simply dragging the dead weight of the boat. Walter ties one end of a heavy rope to the net and the other end of that rope to the truck winch. Down the beach, Mitchell and Wally have done the same with the other end of the net that we let go. The winch winds up the rope, pulling net in with it. One or two people, depending on how many hands show up on any given day, pile up the net, freeing it of tangles as it is winched in. When the rope that is pulling the net reaches the truck, the stacker in the truck unties it and the rope is walked to the water and tied onto the next segment of net, which is then winched in. This is repeated until all of the wings have been recovered.

As the net comes in, the trucks drive toward one another. Vic positions himself and his gear about fifteen yards down the beach from where the bag full of fish will be hauled onto the sand. Finally, after fifteen minutes or so of hauling, the only part of the net that remains in the water is the bag at its center. All of the catch has been driven into it. When both ends of the net are secured, the winches start to pull in the bag.

Now comes the moment of truth . . . the catch. As Vic explained to me when we had a beer and a chat two weeks ago, the ocean is a "black box": You don't know what's there, what's going to come into your net until you finally heave it on shore with your catch, floppingly alive, in front of you.

As we all drag the full bag above the high water mark, we see that it isn't much of a haul. There are fifty or sixty rays, which Jens and Mickey keep for lobster bait, a few middling bluefish and a handful of stripers without the wit to stay with their school. Vic counts it as a dry run, not a real haul.

As with any less than successful fishing, the haul seiners pool their wisdom about what went wrong. The consensus is that the tide was running a little strong so that our lead weights bounced off the bottom and the fish were able to escape.

Eastward the tide is less advanced. We drive the beach. The swells are a bit fatter, but still not enough to scrub the mission. Nevertheless, as a greenhorn, they don't want me on the boat. "Too rough," Jens says.

The engine revs, Walter pops her into gear and the truck stalls. "Old motor, older transmission," Walter explains. On the next try he gets up a fair amount of speed. The transmission slips, the dory slides, hesitates and teeters off the truck.

We reload. Third time charmed: Jens and Mitchell climb the face of a breaking swell, clear it and the net pays out. I stay on shore with Mickey, the class clown of the crew, the Vietnam vet. He is a born gabber and I am content to listen.

"My family were the lighthouse keepers at the Point," he says with pride.

I'm impressed. "What did they do on the job?"

"Actually, nothing much. You just sit on your ass and look out for whatever."

When he is not seining, he tells me, he tends nets with Jens on Gardiners Bay. They get some bass, tons of squid (literally tons). They scallop in the short season when the delectable bay scallops fetch $18 a pound wholesale. He does carpentry, works construction. He gets by.

Mickey calls my attention to the chop on the water. It has grown since early morning. The wind is rising and it's cold. Mickey swears he sees snow squalls on the horizon where the bleached-out sun breaks through the cloud cover and lights up a patch of ocean.

Jens comes on shore. We rush over to see what the ocean has given up this time. There are, by my estimate, a couple of hundred bass, a few dozen blues and skates, half as many flounder and one big weakfish which the crew offer to me. They keep the rest of the catch except for the stripers. They will be returned to the sea. There is nothing exceptional about this haul except for one monster bass. It's the hugest striper I have seen in many years.

We all stand in awe of the big bass.

"Haven't seen one of those in a while," Jens says, "she's a beauty."

Vic carries the bass to the holding tank where he keeps the

fish that he will tag. The tank is made of plastic, 4 x 4 x 6. He fills it with seawater by means of a pump that he runs into the surf. His team sets a plywood board over one end of the tank to serve as a work surface. On the board he sets a scale for weighing and measuring length.

Vic dips a net into the tank, pulls out a striper and places it on the scale. His assistant calibrates the scale and then takes the weight. Vic scrapes two scales off the fish and places them in an envelope. The number on the envelope corresponds to the number on the plastic tag that he inserts just behind the dorsal fin. Some time, at some place on the Atlantic Coast, another fisherman will catch one of these fish and report its capture to the 1–800 number on the tag. In this way, one fish at a time, scientists are developing a profile of the striped bass—its range, its habits, its survival.

As the first order of business, Vic wants to get the big cow weighed, measured, scaled and back in the water as soon as possible. She (bass this size are almost always females) could very well turn out to be the biggest fish of the year. I had always heard that the really big fish come at the end of the autumn run.

"What's this one doing here with these little guys?" I ask.

"Big fish are different," Vic answers. "They have different needs, different ways of moving. They don't follow a set pattern. They don't necessarily migrate the same as the smaller fish. They can tolerate cooler temperatures so they can stay later, so maybe they just stay around the rips until they feel the need to go back to wherever they're going. If it's the Hudson or the Chesapeake they know they can make it in two days, whereas the younger fish are just taking off and probably don't know where they are going.

"Big fish take their time and do what they want. It's like the old joke about the bull and the young bull standing on top of the mountain, looking down at all of the cows. The young bull says, 'Let's run down there and screw one of those cows.' And the old bull says, 'Don't sell yourself short pardner, let's *walk* down there and screw *all* of them.' "

"What do you think she weighs?" I request that everyone make a guess. The estimates range from forty-five to maybe fifty pounds.

Vic measures the length—forty-eight inches. His assistant, Heidi, takes a reading on the scale. The digital readout cycles until it stops at thirty-eight pounds. No one has guessed right and therein lies a lesson. Fish tales don't happen because fishermen consciously lie. They happen for the same reason that a parent thinks that his child is prettier, more musical or a better athlete than he or she really is. Our emotions color our reality. When you are the fisherman, good fish always become great fish: not because you are lying, but because that's the way it felt, that's the way you saw it. Accurate weights and measures are not the stuff of angling tales.

We marvel at the beauty of the big bass. Vic lifts her from the tank as he would a sleeping child from the back seat of a car. He wades thigh-high into the surf and puts her in the water. She swims a short way and turns on her side, tail flipping; she struggles. Vic follows after her, a swell breaks against him, soaking him. No matter, he reaches the bass, rights her, and she swims slowly in the shallows. She regains her strength, turns away from the shore and swims off. We see her head and tail as she moves through the first line of breakers. Then she is gone.

# October 11: The Dude

≋

IF DIXON IS THE KING OF THE HILL, the guy who has won his spurs and feels no need to show off, Dave Blinken is the Young Gun, the talented hotshot still out to impress. Paul's SeaCraft is understated, nothing flashy, built to handle strong seas. David's twin-engine racing green Contender, with its high, raked prow, is the NASCAR muscle car, as it were, to Paul's classic roadster. Paul dresses in khaki, jeans and a fishing bandana, everything sun faded. Blinken, on a warm day, looks like the laid-back dude with the cool sunglasses who rents surfboards. When it's cold, the surfer becomes an au courant playboy skier. Paul comes from money, old California, *non-showbiz* money. Dave, too, comes from money—East Coast, Upper-East-Side-with-a-big-house-in-the-Hamptons money.

There has been little love lost between them since David started guiding the same waters and some of the same clients as Paul. I have never fished with David, so I have mainly seen him through Paul's eyes until this year. Now I see him every day, working hard, getting to the fish. He's good. I want to check him out.

The weather is not as cold as yesterday. It should go back up to the mid-sixties, although once again the wind is blowing a ton, west 15 with gusts to 30.

David says, "Piece of cake, my boat can handle it."

Young gun bravado, or am I unreasonably timid about wind and waves?

"Meet me at my boat, we'll check it out."

A half hour later I am at Star Island Marina, near the mouth of the harbor. From our vantage point you can see spray breaking over the western wall of the inlet. Dave is not concerned. Well, maybe a little concerned. We decide to drive to the Point to check it out. There are not many surfcasters around, usually a sign that there is not a blitz.

Off the Point, we see Paul's boat, slowly cruising, searching. Bob Sullivan is also there in his skiff—poor bastard! Dave wants to give it a try. I'm game. At the dock, Dave has invited a friend along, Peter Rothwell. He looks familiar, then I place him.

"Mid September out on Gardiners Bay," I say, "fishing albies off Accabonac Neck. I was in a canoe. You came over in a flats boat and we talked. You caught albies by the black buoy."

"You're right. I keep a boat out here and take four weeks off from work and fish every day. I pulled the boat yesterday and I'm out of here tomorrow. Welcome to my farewell party."

Blinken starts his engines and we take off for the Point. The wind at our backs doesn't bite like it did yesterday. The sun has warmed up again, too. The waves are big are the north side, but Blinken had it right about his boat: It moves powerfully and smoothly.

Paul sees us. I have already told him that I was "sleeping around" with David today. He calls on the radio.

"All right boys, looks like you timed it right. Here comes the first blitz of the day."

We are by the Sewer Pipe. The fish are working about two hundred yards offshore underneath the gulls. We haven't found bass so far away from shore this season, so we think it must be albacore, but as we near them, we see the Black Hole. The bass have pinned the bait against the rip. Around them, like the sparks flying off of a pinwheeling firecracker, big bluefish pick at the edges of the bait school.

David cuts the engines. We drift down on the school. Peter is in the bow. I take the stern. He lets go a forehand cast. I release a backcast. He hits the center of the school and comes tight to a bass. I hang a bluefish that fights like a mean drunk before he cuts me off. I would fish with a wire leader all the time in these conditions, but the guides have a thing—a taste and style thing—about wire leaders. It's what "meat fishermen" use. In my experience, fish, when they are in such a frenzy, won't notice; but style is important so I don't argue. While I tie on a new fly, an enormous striper breaks water ten feet from the boat. I could have hit it with my rod tip, but I am not ready and Rothwell is still fighting his bass so we do not present a fly to it. Goddamn!

As we approach the rip, a bait school darkens and rises quickly. Lazily swimming through them, the white and green sides of the albacore show. They act as if they have all the time in the world. The rainbait know, on the other hand, that they may have little time left to them so they rush right and left, up and down. A chain of rainbait, like arcing water from a garden hose, flies through the air. We cast at every boil, but the albies will not take. Had we been quicker, right on them, then maybe.

Rothwell has an explanation. "There's a sweet spot in a school of albacore. If I can get in there right away with one or two false casts, I feel I have a chance . . . unless I'm standing on my line when I release my cast. I do that a lot."

Good notion, the sweet spot in the school. Everything has a sweet spot. There's a sweet spot on a tennis racket, a sweet spot on a baseball bat about six inches down from the head, a sweet spot on a chef's knife that seems to cut through an onion all by itself. Fishing has its own sweet spot—just upstream of the outermost ripple of the riseform of a sipping trout, or six feet in front of a mudding bonefish, double that for cruising tarpon. The sweet spot of a school of albacore is just off its center cheating toward the direction in which they are moving.

Just then, the bass come up behind us in the cove where the clear western tide meets the pellucid green rip. We start our drift over the white sandy bottom. Below us, the dark forms of bass; at that depth there is a hint of purple in them. They disappear from sight where the water changes color. We let our flies sink. I *know* there is a fish there, but I can't see it. It hits in between my strips. I react and slam the hook home, moving my rod tip to the right and pulling hard on the line with my left hand—a strip strike. The bass runs into the rip. We follow. I thrust my rod tip right then left, over and over, tiring the fish quickly. He comes to hand and I release him.

Now two schools erupt right under the lighthouse. The birds zero in, the surfcasters, too. The scampering fishermen look like the Lilliputians hard at work tying up Gulliver. With the sun in the west, the arching fishing lines all in the air at once look like a cobweb falling. We can't get within striper range, though. Too close to the rocks.

The sea monster that we pulled up in the haul seine yesterday is still on my mind. "What's the biggest striper you caught on a fly," I ask David.

"Does it count if I didn't catch it but it was on my boat?"

"If you're a guide, probably more."

"We were out on the flats. That's what makes it really special. To me the flats are more intellectual and demanding than the blitz."

"Amanda thinks the same."

"I'm not surprised. It's a different game. Anyway, the guy shows up on my boat—completely hung over, his eyelids just about pasted shut. I stand him in the bow and he kind of sways there and moans every now and again. 'Oh brother,' I tell myself, 'this is going to be a long day.'

"Just then I see a huge shadow near the boat. I tell the guy he is going to get one cast and since he can't cast that far, I tell him to wait and don't move till I cue him. He gets off a sloppy, half roll cast, half water haul, but it lands in front of the fish. The fish turns, inhales the fly and the adrenaline gets my angler moving. The fish runs all over the flat. Finally, I grab it with my Bolga grips [a device that holds but does not injure a fish]. We measure him at forty-two inches. Biggest I ever took. I'm out every day, all day, this guy parties all night, drinks his brains out, stumbles on my boat and gets the fish of a lifetime."

"Look at it as a tribute to your guiding ability."

"Yeah, whatever. I don't really remember big fish as well as I remember first fish. The first one of a species always sticks in my mind. First bonefish, first trout and the first tarpon—that was an experience. When it jumped, it hit the water like a piano dropping out of an airplane."

"Nice turn of phrase, Captain. I don't really remember first fish. I remember special times and places."

"Like for instance?"

"One time I was in India to write a travel show. We stayed

at the Lake Palace of Udaipur: It was the evil heroine's head-quarters in the James Bond movie *Octopussy*. Gorgeous place, all white, a classic Moghul building. The Maharana, some centuries back, had built it for his harem.

"There is a large statue of a goddess, bare breasted, about twenty feet from the end of the palace island. One night, I heard little kisses in the water around the waist of the goddess. I had my four-piece rod with me, so I strung it up and tied on a little deer hair bug that my friend Jack Allen—the Everglades bass guide—gave me. It works great with bream and bass. I had no idea what was swimming around the thighs of the goddess. Jack Allen had taught me to cast up against the coral outcropping in the Everglades and to let my bug fall on the water, the same way that a natural—a beetle or a cricket—might fall off a tree or bush.

"I cast softly, aiming straight for the deity's cleavage. The fly stopped when it hit her breastbone, fell into the water, and the Lake Udaipur version of a sunfish rose to it. It was five inches, a real nothing, but I caught her off the bosoms of a goddess. I remember that little fish much better than ten thousand others, much bigger."

My once-upon-a-time tale is interrupted by the cough of static and the Brooklynese of Tommy Cornicelli on the radio.

"Get your ass over here, Blinken."

"Where?"

"Where do you think? North side. They're everywhere. Stop talking and move."

We round the Point as Tommy suggested, and the albacore are still up, but the bass explosion that summoned us is, for the moment, over. They will be back. The tide is right. The bait is in the water.

We wait. I practice my backcast. David says I turn my body too much before I release it. I have always thought of myself as a good civilian caster, kind of like a good club golfer. I am learning that this is a comforting illusion. The more I'm out here, the more evident it is that my skills want perfecting. The average fisherman, who doesn't get the chance to be on the water every-day, is usually so caught up in the excitement of getting to go fishing, and actually seeing fish, that he or she has little time to reflect on the fine points of the cast. For the first time in a good twenty years, I have time for everything: spending a month with a flyrod in your hand will teach you your failings and, if you are ready to work, do wonders for your casting . . . and your soul.

David pulls the cork on a bottle of merlot. He has turned out to be a much more laid-back fisherman than I had thought, tres mellow. But then, everything is mellow at sundown on the ocean. The flyrod fleet gathers for a gam. David fills some plastic cups with wine and passes them around.

The sun goes fiery gold in the west, the Striper Moon, still two days from full, peeks over the waves. It grows, as orange as a fat, ripe pumpkin. We bob in the riptide as the moon climbs higher and puts some sky between itself and the horizon. Then the bass show. It is as if the moon is tied to the sea by a string, and as it rises it pulls up an acre of bass. They feed furiously, slapping the water with their tails, their chomping like the roar of a Roman stadium, all voices clamoring for a kill. The moon inches still higher and the black shadow on the water grows. There are thousands of fish frothing, more than an acre, maybe ten acres, maybe the whole ocean.

Although there is more inanimate matter than there are living things on earth, at times like this one remembers that our small blue planet is more full of life than a billion, or a trillion, or an unnumberable collection of bare rocks in our universe. Our third rock from the sun, where acres of bass and miles of birds take center stage, is alive and teeming with things that move, eat, love, fight and flyfish.

We jump to our posts fishing to the tom-tom beat of a thousand bass knocking against the sides of our boat. The moon is so bright that we can see the bait wads, like silvery moon shadows flecked with foam.

### Later October 11: State of the Run

At dinner, I report to Paul about the acre of bass. He had already gone in for the day when it happened.

"That's the essence of the bass in the fall. It's a force of nature that people rarely see. My guys on the boat today and yesterday, they'd never seen this. They just sat there in awe and I'm yelling, 'Cast! Cast!' You literally have to tap them on the shoulder and say, 'You've got to start casting !' But they can't concentrate on what you're saying because their eyes are focused on this massive horde of fish and they've never seen anything like it. They can't concentrate enough to cast. They sit there stunned, literally stunned."

Today the fishing pattern appeared to change. I ask Paul about it.

"We saw schools of bass way outside today, does that mean they are moving off the Point, and The Run is over?"

"I think we're okay," he reassures me. "What happens with the west wind is, it's pushing bait away from the Point and the tide is taking it out. It's moving it offshore basically. What we want is a nice condition with northwest winds pushing the bait into the north side between Montauk and Shagwong. Then the bait moves around the Point to the southside, which is why we have it sitting in Turtle Cove and the surf gets brown with it all the way down into Caswell's and Ditch Plains. As long as the bait holds, the bass won't leave.

"The weather pattern for the next few days is going to tell what's going to happen with the rest of the season. It will either be great guns and it will build and build and the albacore will come back out of the rips and back inshore or you may see the albacore tail off. If the albacore tail off, then you've got a water temperature thing and the bait will start tailing off and the bass will follow."

"But then," I ask, "we'll still get the big fish, won't we, Paul? Vecchio says the migration really rages when the temperature drops below fifty-four degrees."

"He's right . . . if we hit the herring run like we used to, remember?"

I remember. Paul is referring to December 8, 1994, when he and I caught thirty odd fish in the thirty-six-inch class. People who were there still recall it as the blitz of a lifetime. But that is not the Autumn Run per se. As both he and Vic have explained, there are plenty of big fish in the rips, but they don't come in for the rainbait on the shore. They don't need to. There is rainbait over the rips, also spider crabs, bunker and squid.

Paul continues, "The big fish come with the big bait, *if* the big bait, herring, shows up. The herring draw them down the coast with them. The fish that we have now, generally speaking, are not huge fish, not compared to the fish that are in the rips. They're not the thirty to fifty pounders. We're in the juvenile class, the ten to twenty-five pounders—and the twenty-five pounder is a trophy for flyfishing. When the rainbait gets as big and dark as it was today, though, there's the possibility of some better fish like the mongos we hit the other day off of Turtle Cove. We got some that were probably up to thirty pounds, but normally you need big bait in the surf to bring big fish into the surf."

If the big guys are in the rips, you might ask, why don't we flyfishermen go out to the rips for the them? The answer is, it is not all about big. Everyone wants to catch big fish, but catching them on top when you can see them is what every flyrodder prefers. At this time of year you will find them consistently on top in the shallow water by the shore.

"When I was with Levison," I interject, "we saw silver herring beach themselves. That would have brought big fish up, wouldn't it?"

"Generally speaking, yes," Paul answers, "but even that is not considered big bait. I am talking about bunker and blueback herring that are close to ten to twelve inches long, something that really sparks a fish to go up. When the blueback herring were in strong and the tide went out over the humps—Shagwong, Great Alaska, Great Eastern, the Elbow—up would come the big fish. The birds working above were gannets and they put on a show."

Paul gets up a head of steam as he paints the picture of the gannets—migratory seabirds with a six-foot wingspan. He spreads his arms, rises from his chair, paces up and down the room. This is the heart of what Paul is about. Flyfishing is his "I-Thou" experience with nature. It is an epiphany that comes from being part of the aliveness that fills the air, the sea, his boat.

He continues, "The first gannets to show are not yet mature, they are gray. The parents are white and black; black wing tips, white bodies. Gannets dive from sixty to seventy feet. They spot their prey, they tuck their wings and, right before they hit the water, they take in a gulp of air that fills up these spaces in their neck—shock absorbers that act like a rubber cushion. They hit the water doing fifty miles an hour. They'll go seven feet to ten feet under water, grab the herring and come up. When they fly, they turn in a circle, come around and then dive right back down again. This creates a living white Ferris wheel that moves across the water. You'll have birds fighting bass for the herring. So, you'll have this pushing and pulling with forty-pound bass and huge gannets.

"Because the bass school in year classes, at times like this when every fish is up you can look around and say, 'There's twenty pounders, over there' and then you look to your left and there's maybe fifteen fish flipping up, and then you look over here and maybe there's ten fish and their tails are this wide"—Paul extends his palms and puts them side by side like a shadow puppeteer imitating a bird in flight—"and they're thirty pounders, and then you look over here and there's three fish that are the size of this table. They're all coming out of the rip, they're all chasing the herring and they all stick together. I wish you could count on the herring and the gannets, but since that time with you in '94, I haven't seen them."

We sigh a where-are-the-good-old-days sigh. I have come out here every year since 1994 looking for a repeat of that day, and haven't caught another bass feeding on herring.

Just as there are mayfly hatches that trout fishermen can usually depend on, in Montauk, we count on the rainbait. The Run, the predictable event, coincides with the appearance of the rainbait. When they are in, the fishing is great every day. When the northeasters of November drive them away, The Run dies. If the herring come and the last big boys come up and feed, I look at that like the afterlife: nice if it happens, but I don't count on it. If Paul is right, we are near the peak of The Run. Whether it builds, whether it stays is all a function of weather. One thing for sure, though, it's here now.

# October 12:
# My Non-Rabbit's Foot

≋

I LEFT THE LIGHT BURNING on the porch. Tom Akstens, professor of English, Adirondacks flyfishing guide and my old friend, arrived sometime after 1:00 A.M. His door is still closed when I awake. The Robot says it's going to hit seventy this afternoon with light west winds.

Tom is a good fisherman, I am a good fisherman, but, somehow, over the two and a half decades that we have fished together, we have had, at most, two or three excellent fishing days and the rest have ranged from unmemorable to disastrous. We enjoy ourselves. We laugh long and deeply. But our fishing generally stinks.

If we were slaves of statistics we would never fish together again. But we keep at it. We are two products of the sixties who share the same taste in obscure folkie bands, literature and an abhorrence of living or vacationing near a mall or a franchise. Most of all, Tom, like Josh, is always ready to fish.

Of the three great days that Tom and I have had in our otherwise dispiriting chronicle of fishing adventures, there was one at Turtle Cove. From that experience I take heart that our jinx, though powerful magic, can be overcome by Montauk's mojo.

The first thing you notice about Akstens is how much of him there is. At six-foot-seven he is easily the largest man I know. He played center for Holy Cross in Boston. This was an act of supreme rebellion, because his family of upper-class Boston Irish were mostly Harvard alums. But Harvard had a crummy basketball team so Tom went to Holy Cross where he had the soul-searing experience of guarding Kareem Abdul Jabbar, who was still known by his given name of Lew Alcindor.

"He just went right by me. It was like I was standing still," Aksens will recount, if pressed.

Tom lives in the Adirondacks now. He teaches English at the State University of New York, and guides for trout and bass. Musically and culturally hip, he is in many ways an old-fashioned New Englander who happens to own the latest Macintosh computer. He collects old cameras and old fishing plugs, is a fanatic gardener and is in the habit of finding fishing places that, by the looks of them, were written about in *Field & Stream* in 1920 and haven't changed one jot nor tittle since. Of a piece with his character, he wrote his doctoral dissertation on non-trendy Alexander Pope.

Tom grew up saltwater fishing at the family home on Cape Cod. I still have a set of Manhattan glasses that he gave me when he sold the place. They are short and thin stemmed, with red glass on the bottom and clear, etched crystal on top. They were worn and chipped from years of heavy use when I got them and more so now.

We start late, about midday, with Amanda. Tom, true-to-form, has brought an infinite amount of gear in an equally wondrous number of bags, pouches, cases, waterproof bags and thermoses. He is of the school of anglers that needs to have everything for *every* eventuality. I'm different. I feel like the soul of thoroughness if I remember rod, reel, leader and a few flies. I get a bit of ego-satisfaction out of this minimalism, but I also fish a lot with geared-up professionals, so I end up borrowing this and that as the day goes along.

Fishing with Amanda, we chase some tentative schools of albacore off Shagwong. Tom needs work before he has perfected the necessary quick release from a rocking boat. For that matter, I could use some work, too. The albies are finicky. Amanda says to move on. At worst, there will be other fish not to catch.

Paul is already on the Point, dredging the bottom with his suck 'em up routine. As always, his boat has attracted a retinue. If there are no birds, and no blitzes, the conventional wisdom is follow Paul.

Amanda demonstrates for Tom. She casts and then lets the line sink, explaining, "You let it go to the bottom, start to strip very fast, then pause, then vary the retrieve. The fast strip will get their attention, then you need to let them catch up, then pull it away, and finally they get so pissed they eat it . . . like . . . that . . . fish on!" she gasps. It's nice when the fish read the script, too.

"My nails," she says, pronouncing it "nay-uhls" in her best imitation of a Long Island trophy wife on her first fishing trip, "puhleeze, I spent a fawchun on them at Elizabeth Arden."

Tom, baseball cap turned backward, starts snapping off shots like a fashion photographer. "Work with me baby! Love ya!" he says, camera in one hand, rod in the other. Bang—he has a bass on, too. He puts down the camera and fights the bass. While Amanda plays her fish, I lean over, grab Tom's striper and lip lift it into the boat. We measure him—twenty-six inches. A nice chunky boy.

There are no blitzes showing so we set up south of the rip

and drift across it, part of a line of nine or ten boats doing the same. Little wind, bright sun, a clear cobalt sky, a fish every now and then—the scene is as relaxed as sitting in a farm pond rowboat casting worms on a bobber, talking, not talking, joking, just sitting and staring. Paul comes over and tosses us some macadamia nut–white chocolate chip cookies.

"Man, it's really uncrowded for such nice weather and a Saturday!" Amanda exults.

"Amanda," I correct her, "it's Thursday."

We all take a beat and then explode with laughter. What a guide comment! You're out on the water, day after day, you never watch the news, you glance at the newspaper if there are any left at the store at the end of the day. Guides know the tide, they know what fly to use. Knowing what day of the week it is doesn't enter into the equation.

On the west end of the cove we see darkness on the water. We sneak out of the pack and move toward it. Jack Yee, the "Mayor," spots Amanda and waves us over, leaving no doubt by his hand signals that we have a blitz forming.

Amanda has gained the good will and advice of East Enders who would have barely spoken to her had she been just another male guide on a flats boat. Jack Yee's leading us to fish when every other surfcaster wishes that the flyrod boats would be swallowed by a giant squid is a case in point.

The stripers are feeding in the rocks at the end of the cove. The surfcasters can easily flick their lures a rod's length and be into fish. There is no way, though, for us to navigate among the rocks and the shore fishermen, so we drift east with the tide, back toward the Point.

In the same place and the same stage in the tide as yesterday, we drift over the white sand patch in the center of the bowl formed by Turtle Cove. Twenty bass, then thirty, then a hundred, move under us—a shimmering green shadow in the gin clear tide. Witching water, for sure.

"Oh . . . . . . my . . . . . . God!" Amanda says, two or three times.

"Jesus Christ, would you look at that!" Tom agrees.

We are silent, drifting with the fish, watching them. We don't even cast. They move like a grazing herd of deer. Ken Rafferty, a genial flyrod guide, parallels our drift. His two happy anglers have done well and, to celebrate, light up Cohibas.

"Want a Heineken?" they offer with the largesse that good fishing engenders.

I accept. I didn't know how thirsty I was until that first sip— cold and bracing, delish. A moment later the fish emerge from the foam, tight against the lighthouse rocks.

So much for the beer. I wedge it in the console and grab my rod as our reverie jump-cuts to a burst of action. Fishing, I realize at times like these, is similar in its pace to baseball: Nothing happens for a long time; everyone stands around until someone hits the ball where someone else isn't. In an instant, the static tableau becomes activity in every direction as the fielders chase the ball, the base runners take off, the coaches windmill their arms. Likewise, the lazy pow-wow of boats and the hands-on-hips surfcasters now spring to frenetic life.

We move in on the fish, fifty feet from the rocks. They dive down and rise up, like a flock of pigeons wheeling in the sky before they come in to roost. The revved up surfcasters heave metal to either side of us, aiming a few curses and threats our way. We back off rather than risk being hit by lead or hooked by a lure.

"I've been holding it in all summer," Amanda says as she

leans over the wheel and maneuvers us between rocks, surfcasting lures and even more boats drawn by the raging fish. "One day I am going to say, 'Go fuck yourself,' to the bunch of them!"

I doubt that she will, but if she did it wouldn't do much anyway. "This is where the fish are so this is where the fishermen are and we are going to get in each other's way and get angry but we will all keep doing it. No right, no wrong here, just the way it is. If we don't feel like fighting, we should pack it in for the day," I offer.

Tom is fine with it. Amanda says, "Your call." We decide not to muscle in.

We are in no rush to get back to Gerard Drive, because another angling friend, Mark Sedotti, is due on the 7:45 train at Amagansett. We stop for a drink at the Shagwong Tavern on Main Street in Montauk. Like many of the buildings in present-day Montauk, the Shagwong was built by Carl Fisher, the same larger-than-life character who built the Indianapolis Speedway and then, with his auto fortune, went on to create Miami Beach out of 3,500 acres of mosquito-infested mangroves that made up the barrier island between Miami and the Atlantic. Flush with the millions that his real estate venture had brought him in the South, Fisher's next project was to be "the Miami of the North," Montauk.

In 1925, for $2,500,000 he bought all ten thousand acres of the current village of Montauk. In place of the few fishermen's huts without benefit of electricity or plumbing, he envisaged an upper-class playground with yacht clubs, polo grounds, casinos, restaurants . . . the works.

He built the palatial Montauk Manor—high on a hill: its faux Tudor lines suggest an apartment building designed by Henry VIII. Right off of the village green he built his headquarters, the six-story Montauk Improvement Building, which was at that time the tallest building on Long Island. For a brief period Montauk became a society destination.

In 1927, Fisher's dreams began to crumble when a great hurricane hit Miami and collapsed the real estate market upon which his fortune depended. What that hurricane didn't take, the stock market crash of 1929 harvested. Any gleanings that were left behind were washed away in the hurricane that hit Montauk in 1938. The town wasn't destroyed, but high society retreated for good.

The present-day Shagwong Tavern is still the classic watering hole for serious anglers. The dark wood panelling; the walls that may have been white about 200,000 Lucky Strikes ago; the friendly and pretty Irish barmaids (Montauk has always been a cops and firemen resort favored by New York City Irish); the swordfish head jutting out from the wall as if it had rammed through it on a high tide; the dollar bill impaled on the swordfish's nose; the pictures of generations of smiling anglers with swordfish, sharks and stripers of such great size that they required no exaggerated measurements. The back wall photos of Jackie Kennedy in summery Capri pants, sexy and at ease. My bourbon old-fashioned, ordered single and poured double. The apres-fish patrons still sporting their daytime sweatshirts, two-day stubble and jeans with stains that could easily be bluefish blood accented with a dollop of striper scales—the Shagwong Tavern fits seamlessly with the spirit of the Autumn Run.

The stock market ticker runs across the bottom of the bar's TV. The last time I fished at Montauk with Tom, the stock market tanked: the day of the Great Crash of 1987. Today, in spite of our "jinx," the Dow maintained its relentless climb.

A sign of grace?

# October 13:
# The Artful Caster

TODAY I GET TO PLAY CAPTAIN. With the arrival of Mark Sedotti last night, we are now a party of three: too many for a flats skiff and all of the bigger boats have charters. Sedotti is the greatest caster I have ever seen and an innovative fly tier. Mark now works in the fishing industry as casting teacher cum adviser cum expert-at-large for the Scott Flyrod company. When I first met him he was a paralegal with ultra flexible hours. This allowed him to fish when he wanted. I used to think of Sedotti as the Medieval townie of flyfishing, the guy who hung around the university, translating the forgettable tracts of big shot professors while he did something really important on his own—like discovering zero.

We get a start that is neither late nor early (about 10:00) and stop at the store for sandwiches (ham and cheese on a kaiser roll, mustard, mayo, lettuce and "real" tomatoes from a local farm). The headline in the *Times* concerns the firestorm of violence consuming Israel and its occupied territories. Page one carries a banner headline, the kind you might see for an assassination or declaration of war. The color photo shows a crowd of angry

Palestinians in a trophy-like display of the corpse of an Israeli soldier they have beaten to death.

The event and the sharp prose shake me like news of the death of a relative. For three weeks I have felt that there are two worlds: The one that I live in now starts in Amagansett and ends about a half mile off the Point. Everything else—New York, the Middle East, butchery in Africa, AIDS in Asia—is another world, one that I am not part of. That flyfishing enables me to maintain this two-worlds illusion most of the time is one of its great balms.

Through I-don't-want-to-get-out-of-bed-for-six-weeks depressions, through low funds, the break-up of relationships, deaths in the family, I have always been able to flyfish and while I am fishing, all of these things fly out of my life. The minute I am off the water, they return in force, but while I have a rod in my hand and can wave the line in the air so that I feel that I am physically touching the world at the other end of the line, the act of fishing banishes sadness.

Once, when I crashed out of a ten-year relationship, I was lower than I have ever been, a basket case. It took me two weeks to write a story for *Sports Afield* that I should have knocked off in a day. I would sit at the typewriter (pre-computer days), struggle through a sentence and then start bawling. If I weren't writing about fishing I doubt that I could have forced out even those few sentences. My friends in Sun Valley invited me to come up and fish. I stayed in a buddy's garage, in a sleeping bag next to his motorcycle. Every day, I got up and fished and every day, while I was fishing, my sadness left. It wasn't even remotely there.

These are rather somber thoughts for the start of a fishing

day, but the newspaper got to me. I resurface when we pull into Uhlein's boat livery in Montauk where we have found a Parker (same make as Levison's).

The weather should be nice—high about seventy with northwest winds 7 to 12. The boat looks great, but once out of the harbor, we realize that rental boats are the seagoing version of those fully furnished apartments that guys move into after their wives catch them cheating and kick them out. This boat, like those apartments, does its job, but it does not feel lived-in, personally owned. Oh well, this kind of fishing isn't rocket science, or even boat driving science. We know the fish are at the Point. All we need to do is drive there and then, since I have learned where the rocks and shoals are, we can probably avoid those. We have a radio. Paul is out there. We'll find fish.

We lumber through the rip at Shagwong and on to Montauk. Slack tide, nothing happening. Most of the gulls stand on the beach taking the sun like a bunch of old Russians reading the paper and chatting on the boardwalk at Brighton beach. The surf fishermen likewise sit on rocks, lean against their cars, stand in chatting groups.

We start at Caswell's and drift back to the Point. Tom shoots pictures, Mark casts. Quiet time. The sibilance of Mark's line racing through the guides says *good cast, good cast, good cast.* Seated, with very little physical exertion, he throws the line half again as far as I can standing when I put my whole body into it. A well-cast flyline looks like a wave approaching the shore—a moving curl with a lengthening trail, the physical track of force in motion.

He flicks his backcast with the ease that you or I might pick a petal from a flower and toss it behind us. Tom and I look at

Mark, look at each other and exclaim a wonder-filled "holy shit."

The calm water changes character in an instant as bass, in a fifty-yard circle, come to the surface. Tom, who sees things first through his telephoto lens, calls out before the Black Hole breaks the surface. Mark gets off a cast immediately. I try to, but my line has been coiled on the deck for so long that it is tangled and I develop a knot that prevents me from casting. Mark's cast, on the other hand, hits the bull's eye. His line tightens, the rod bends and, finally, Mark decides it's time to stand up. He whips the fish quickly.

We move further out on the rip. In front of us, right on the current wall of the rip, the bait turns the water brownish red, but mostly red. The bait are crazed. Their predators are in no hurry. First a handful of blues lope through, then bass, gently twisting, then albacore doing the fish version of a show horse's sideways canter. The baitfish leap like a corps de ballet made up of fat silvery raindrops.

We cast. We catch nothing.

Paul signals. He mouths the word "bass" and with the slightest hand signal and nod of his head, indicates where they are. Very leisurely, so as not to draw attention, he leaves the pack of boats that are mesmerized by uncooperative albacore. When we arrive between the Sewer Pipe and the Radar Tower no more than twenty feet from shore, the bass are on top again. Better yet, we have them all to ourselves. I am at the wheel. Tom casts from the bow and gives a joyful yawp as he drives the hook home. Mark, likewise, proceeds to catch fish after fish like a methodical and highly practiced hitman. Not an ounce of wasted motion.

Within minutes our private school becomes the property of

a dozen boats. Many of them are owned by the people who have hosted me this month—Amanda, Bob Sullivan, Paul, Jim Levison, Dave Blinken, Jim Clark. I am quite aware of the etiquette of taking your place in line, never cutting off someone who is moving in on fish, repositioning your boat so that anglers with a fish on don't foul in my prop or cross our lines.

But between being aware of something and being able to handle the boat properly there is a gap in my abilities as a helmsman. A muscular sea gremlin wants to push my boat faster then the other boats so that the only way that I can avoid messing up our synchronized flyfishing fleet is by starting the engine—but that is a no-no because an idling engine will ultimately break up the bait school.

If looks could speak, the phrase that the regulars would utter in chorus would be "Leave the boat handling to the grownups." As the month goes on, however, I will learn that even though my boat handling is not up to pro levels, the everyday guides have the same attitude toward one another. What it comes down to is, "I'll give you room but if I see fish and you see fish and I can't get to them because of you, then you don't know the first thing about handling a boat." The nautical glut is a little much for me. We have had our fill so we exit.

I turn to Sedotti. "Mark, the harbor should be dead calm. Would you mind a casting lesson?" My last lesson was twenty-seven years ago on the Beaverkill River, and all I have had since are a few mid-career corrections from Paul Dixon and Jack Allen, the Everglades largemouth guru.

"Love to," he says. We pass through the mouth of the harbor at Gin Beach. Where the entry channel widens into the harbor proper, we cut the engines. We are protected from any wind. The water is a golden mirror, in the late afternoon sun. If you have any halcyon memories of someone teaching you some-thing—your dad showing you how to ride a bike, your mom showing you how to make a pie crust—in your mind's eye you often see things in this light (as do sappy movies).

It's great to have a patient teacher with us. Trying to learn flycasting from a book is like trying to make love from an anatomy text. It will tell you where, but cannot teach you how. Flycasting is 80 percent of flyfishing, and 90 percent of the cast is feel and touch. There are numerous metaphors that have assisted me in understanding elements of the cast: "The motion is like pulling a drawer open and then sliding it shut," or "The finish is like forcefully driving a thumbtack into a cork board." These are all helpful models, but all models, all metaphors are useful in that they *help* explain a thing, they are not the thing itself. You must play a tune, taste a wine, cook a steak, drive a car before the models and metaphors make any sense. And once you do, you must keep at it and keep thinking about what you are doing in order to improve. Most anglers treat flycasting like bike riding: you learn it once, they think, and that's that.

Saltwater flyfishing—on a boat, in the wind, at a distance—requires more casting prowess then presenting a dry fly to a trout sipping a mayfly forty feet away. It is a powerful tennis game compared to the badminton of trout fishing. The long-range physics of the cast are critical on saltwater: larger flies, heavier lines, longer distance, which translates into mass, velocity and distance—three variables central to any physics equation. In flycasting the variables are all greater on salt water than they are in most freshwater situations. That is why Paul often tells me, frustratedly, how he will frequently have fishermen on board who have been on every blue-ribbon trout stream in the world, yet firing off a sixty-foot cast on command and on target in a boat is impossible for them. Paul gives them great shots at trophy fish and yet they cannot get the fly where it needs to be.

I am an autodidact on the salt: good enough that I can catch enough fish to satisfy myself and most guides. But it is only since I have been out on the water every day that I realize my limitations. Eagerly, I pick up the rod as Mark tells me, "Cast a couple of times. Let me see what you do."

I cast sixty or seventy feet. I double-haul, a technique, necessary in distance casting, where you pull on the flyline with your free hand just before you come forward with your casting stroke. The double haul loads up, i.e., bends the rod more and adds distance to your cast. Mark considers my form.

"You need to come over the top in a throwing motion," he tells me. This runs counter to everything I have ever said to anyone trying to learn to flycast. A major sin, especially with boys who grow up throwing baseballs, is trying to throw the line. While that may be true for the beginning caster, Mark explains that the advanced intermediate (which is me, I hope) will gain a lot by extending the arm, as one does in a good throwing motion. You must remember when you do this to move your rod as if it were a continuation of your arm.

"What you need to do is always be conscious of the rod bending through its whole length. If you try to make it bend, think about it bending all the way to your hand, you will slow down your stroke and build up speed."

This is a good mental model. Too often the caster sees the line straighten out and he or she then stops the stroke, losing all the momentum that would develop if the rod were allowed to flex. Most of us try to make up for this lack of momentum by speeding up our forward cast to hurry the line. That never works. Your arm cannot move far enough fast enough to affect the end of the line one hundred feet from your wrist.

Mark has another, more subtle, piece of advice. "Lead with your reel," he counsels. In other words, if you let the reel come forward of the rest of the rod during your stroke, the line will pull on the rod flexing it fully. At the last moment, when your arm is extended, you flip your wrist over and this will accelerate the line motion, and give you more distance.

Don't take my word for it. If you can cast a flyrod, go out on the lawn and keep thinking about leading with your wrist. You will understand it more fully than reading my description.

One more thought, Charlie Lau, the greatest hitting coach in modern baseball (and a fellow flyfisherman), once told me, "Think the ball up the middle of the infield. If you do that, the homeruns will come on their own." So, too, think of the end of your flyline. That is what you are trying to move. The rod in your hand just gets you there.

Here endeth the lesson.

# October 14:
# Coming through the Rye

≋

ON SATURDAYS, the rules change as weekenders crowd the Point. News of The Run has spread up and down the coast and an armada of boats has descended on "our stretch" of water (you fish a place long enough and you come to think of it as yours). There are boats too big to fish in shallow water, boats too small to fish the rip. No matter—the heavy boats court disaster in close to the rocks and the small guys tempt the waves on the rip. The etiquette book that the guides try to follow—most of the time, unless they are fish crazed—is put aside in favor of an anarchist tract. Rules of the road? There are none. Cutting the other guy off? Sure. Crowding another boat into the rocks? Hey man, sorry, didn't see you.

Sunshine, a light breeze, temperature in the low seventies. Josh, Tom, Amanda and I crowd her little skiff—a tight squeeze but we're all family. We deal with the overpopulated Point by heading west to look for blitzes. There is a mini-blitz by the Warhol estate. Not big, but all ours. Josh takes the bow and with diffident casts, catches four bass. We move over a white patch, the kind where I have come to expect to see bass. They do not disappoint. A herd of a hundred stripers, all big, glides under us.

Amanda, Tom and I have seen this before. Josh hasn't. He looks
in wonderment and sits down. "Jesus Christ!" he says.

Although we haven't yet caught fish in this situation,
Amanda has an idea. "They look like tarpon, let's treat them
like tarpon. Let's sit here until they pass us by, really give it some
time before we start the motor. Then I am going to idle out of
here, swing outside and move into the next cove. If you look
at their path, they have to come around the point at Caswell's
like tarpon coming down a flat. Then we know one of two
things is going to happen. They are going to pin bait against the
point and blow up into a blitz, big time, or they are going to
keep cruising until they find bait. If they cruise, they will go
over the next white patch, because that's the shortest path to the
next cove."

She starts the engine quietly. Just as quietly, throwing no
wake, she turns seaward and circles around to the next white
spot. She points the bow toward the fish. "Strip your line, check
the coils so there's no tangles, get enough line out of the tip,
don't screw around with false casts," she directs.

I strip out fifty feet of line and lay it on the deck, pull another
ten feet through the guides, and hold the weighted fly in my
free hand. This is tarpon technique: get your line ready, make
sure you are not stepping on it and have enough line out of the
rod tip so that you can false cast once, double haul for dear life
and get on the fish quickly.

Amanda stands on the poling platform in the stern of the
boat. From this height, about twelve feet, she can see fish
coming from far away. The sun is still high in the east and the
stripers are coming from the west. Visibility will be perfect on
the white flat.

"Okay, I think I see dark shapes. Yes! Fish! Don't cast until

I tell you. I am going to point the bow toward the shore so we can both cast." This maneuver accommodates her left-handed and my right-handed casting motion.

When the fish are a hundred feet ahead of us Amanda gives the order, "Lay it out there. It's an eleven o'clock shot. Let the fly sink to the bottom and when they come over it, start your strip, the suck 'em up. Go!"

Remembering my lesson of last night, I extend my arm, slow my cast and punch it out there, no tournament winner but a good, long one for me. Amanda descends from the platform and picks up her rod. Her low and slow stroke bends her rod in a reverse letter C. She gives it an easy haul and shoots ten feet past me. We let the flies sink and start our retrieves—fast, hesitate, then erratic. I turn a fish. He chases my fly.

"Slow, slow," Amanda counsels. She looks from her fly to mine and back to hers. She fishes while she directs me. "Tease him, then let him have it."

The fish strikes. I hit it back, but pull the fly out of its mouth. No big deal: Our position makes for a hard hooking angle. The cool thing is we tried something new and I got the fish to eat. Amanda takes the next shot. Her touch is more true than mine in some way I can't quite make out.

"Tom," I say, "there's kind of a Latin rhythm to the suck 'em up strip. I can't put my finger on what it is, can you?"

"I'll think about it," he says.

"C'mon, c'mon eat the fly," Amanda says. Then she breathes deep, drives the hook into a fish, lifts her rod and barks, "Yess!!" She holds the line taut enough to provide some resistance as the fish runs, then she hits the reel, spinning the spool so that it takes up the remaining coiled slack from the deck.

She turns and smiles. "Man, I love it when I get to spank the reel that way. Go fish!"

The bass surrenders after a spunky fight. Amanda lifts it by the lip, pulls the fly out, gives the fish a kiss and releases it. "Get back in there guy."

"Hold on, and sit down," Amanda directs and jams the throttle down full. There are no bass showing. In the distance, birds and white slashes mean we've got albacore about three hundred yards outside the Point, and no other boats are there yet. We fairly fly to the first pod.

"Be ready. Nobody has touched this school. I am not going to give you a forehand shot. It's going to be a backcast. When I cut the engines, get up on the bow and hit them."

Amanda shuts the engines. We approach the pod ahead of our bow wave.

"Take it when you feel you can do it," she says.

Now it's up to me. I turn with my back to the school, double haul and release my backcast. Zing! On target right in the sweet spot of the school. As I turn forward, a fish hits, I strike. This is my first long cast/backcast albacore and I love him for taking my fly and fighting me.

With amusement, we watch three shirtless, shaven-head buddies trolling heavy metal lures from the deck of a cabin cruiser that flies the flag of Guatemala. They move through the pod of fish and, of course, break it up. No matter; other fish are on the Point now. Amanda revs up again and we are the first boat on the fish.

Ernie French, with whom Amanda has a Hepburn and Tracy kind of mutually needling relationship, drives his SeaCraft on a line that will cut us off from the fish. Ernie is a sweetheart but has a knack for getting uptight when he feels other anglers are crowding him (I was the object of some of his displeasure yesterday with my rental boat).

"You're getting too close to my boat, man," Amanda shouts to Ernie, "back down."

Ernie yields the right-of-way.

Amanda turns to us, "Goddam, that's the first time I have had the balls to say that. I've been wanting to do it for a long time. Feels great!"

"Go, girl," Josh says. Actually it comes out as "go-gir . . . ," because a bluefish hits and takes his line. Josh lifts his rod tip high and hops from foot to foot to clear the coils. For no apparent reason, I hear a Scottish air on my inner jukebox: "When a laddie loves a lassie . . ." Josh's nimble feet and raised rod arm are a fine middle-aged guy's version of a Highland fling. After two minutes of good fighting the blue breaks off.

"You fish Amanda," I tell her. Tom's knee is bothering him so he is content to enjoy the ride for the moment.

I move us into the rip. I give the Guatemalan Navy a wide berth as they continue to troll back and forth, covering every inch of the rip like a salvage ship methodically working a piece of ocean. A kayaker is on a pod and I leave it to him. "Poor son of a bitch had to work so hard to get there, leave him be," I explain.

The bait smear forms in front of us, the reddish cloud rises and the albies go to work. Amanda pushes her casts, seventy to eighty feet. She connects.

Right in front of us Alex Powers uncorks a gorgeous backcast. His companion is a beautiful girl with long blond hair. The bill of her baseball cap sits on line with Alex's cast. Youth, beauty and skill make for a pretty composition, which Tom records with half a roll of film. Two monarch butterflies pas de deux through our tableau and my inner jukebox keeps on playing imaginary bagpipes. *No it isn't; those are real bagpipes.* I look up. A piper walks on the cliffs by the lighthouse. A military honor guard is there as well as a bride and groom. It's a weekend wedding party at the Point.

"Coming through the Rye," Tom says in anticipation of my question about the piper's tune.

The bagpipes weave their psychedelic spell on a scene of already considerable sorcery. The air is summer warm. The sea breeze has just a hint of cool in it. The rhythm of false casting, the lines whooshing through the rod guides, patches of foam the size of magic carpets rising with the swell and gliding down their faces, the red clouds of bait that turn and sparkle like ten thousand matches flaring and dying, all contribute to the magic of the moment.

> . . . —*Once again*
> *Do I behold these steep and lofty cliffs,*
> *That on a wild secluded scene impress*
> *Thoughts of more deep seclusion; and connect*
> *The landscape with the quiet of the sky.*

In his heart, Wordsworth must have known Montauk.

Back at the dock, our plan to have a big cook-out at Josh's place on the dunes at Georgica derails when Josh has an alpha wave storm about managing a dinner party. Paul is thrown for a loop because he has already invited his new girlfriend, his ex-mother-in-law and a few other friends.

I am used to cooking in a hurry and for once in my life I have a kitchen and a dining room where ten people coming by for dinner on a few hours' notice doesn't bother me in the least. I offer my services. Paul accepts. In an act of contrition, Josh donates nine well-marbled shell steaks, boned out.

On the way home, Tom and I pull over at Vicki's unattended stand. I flash my lights and she emerges from the kitchen, drying her hands. We exchange pleasantries rapidly as I pick up two heads of freshly picked cauliflower, celery, a shallot and garlic. The cauliflower will be the centerpiece of a roast vegetable platter along with sultana raisins, hot pepper flakes, black greek olives and olive oil. You put it in the oven and forget about it until dinner.

Vegetables taken care of. Meat accounted for. Paul is in charge of desserts. Now for the wine. About a mile from my house, at the junction of Old Stone Highway and Springs Fireplace Road, there is a red A-frame structure, Jacques Franey Wines and Liquors. Jacques is Pierre's son, a young man with Cary Grant good looks, married to and in business with the equally comely Trish Cancalosi. As I greet Jacques, my eyes are drawn to a jeroboam of chianti—the equivalent of six bottles of wine. If you want something that says "party," it's hard to beat a gigantic bottle of wine when guests enter your kitchen. It costs $85—not inconsequential, but the steaks are already bought so after Jacques confirms that it's good wine, I grab it and go.

I have a killer recipe for the steaks from the cookbook of Alain Ducasse, the reigning master chef of France. It calls for a shell steak, coated with brown pepper and salt and basted with lots of butter. On its own that's a fine meal, but the sauce . . . well, that's the thing that puts it over the top.

Like most great sauces, it starts out as a lot of stuff and ends up as a little. Two bottles of red wine, a quart of veal stock, a pound of tomatoes, sour cherries, red wine vinegar, celery, salt, pepper and sugar all reduced to a cup and a half of sauce that is a sweet, tangy and meaty powerhouse.

Between the wine, the steak, the vegetables and two pies from the farmer's market—one peach, one apple—the dinner party is as much fun as the day's fishing. We even talk about other things for a while, but at some point it inevitably gets back to angling

With a little more than three weeks of daily fishing under my belt, I understand how much I didn't see at the beginning of the month. For example, the mysteries of casting and retrieving a fly in pursuit of albacore when they charge in formation. I am puzzled by it. Paul and I step outside for a smoke and he explains.

"When the albacore rush the big pods of rainbait, they line up in formation. They get seven across, seven behind (or ten and ten or twenty and twenty) and they eat their way through the school. It's very methodical. All they have to do is open their mouths and they fill up with bait. It looks great to the fisherman, but you are not going to catch many albies in this situation because your fly has to compete with millions of baitfish. The albacore don't have to chase bait when it is balled up like that, so they sure as hell aren't going to chase your fly either. But *after* the formation of albacore goes through the bait, they break up the bait wad. Now the little stragglers swim frantically to rejoin the group. I call it the 'help me, help me' motion. The albacore start mopping up. That's when you cast. If you can put your fly in front of the fish, maintain a taut line and say, 'help me, help me,' to yourself to set the right stripping rhythm in your head, you have a much better chance of hooking up. Chasing huge clouds of rainbait with the albacore lazily gorging themselves is seductive, but not that productive."

At 11:00 the dinner party, fueled with winish enthusiasm, decides to go to a dance club. I plead my unbreakable (actually nonexistent) routine of early-morning writing. It gets me off the hook. I'm not much of a club guy. They go, I stay. I finish my cigar on the deck, look at the stars and turn in.

# October 15: Calvin Coolidge and His Red Suspenders

≋

IT IS THE WARMEST DAY so far, overcast, almost summery. Josh, Tom and I are on the SeaCraft with Dixon. It is Tom's last day and I am pleased that he has the chance to fish with Paul. Guide-to-guide.

"There aren't many things I could do four days in a row," Tom comments as he casts to a pod of albacore. "Fishing is about all I can think of." Tom has a way of casting and talking where the casting seems a natural part of the conversation. He casts, talks, hooks an albacore, pauses for a second and then continues to tell a tale.

It illustrates the changing nature of fame in celebri-holic America. This is occasioned by our drift past the Warhol cottages and the cliff-top homes of Paul Simon, Mick Jagger and Peter Beard (the renowned photographer of African wildlife). The Hamptons are full of homes of pop culture Olympians, most of them in gated, well-fenced-in property. It wasn't always that way with famous people, Tom says as he begins:

"My grandfather was a judge in Boston, named Thomas Connelly, and he was friends with and an associate of David I. Walsh, who was the governor of Massachusetts and who appointed him judge before he became a U.S. senator. Walsh was a crony of Al Smith and an acquaintance of Calvin Coolidge (my grandfather was also an acquaintance of Coolidge through Governor Walsh).

"There was a strange phenomenon that would happen where Coolidge would leave the White House on his own initiative without telling anyone. He would get on the train and go to Boston. He'd check into the Parker House under his own name. Then he would go to Filene's Basement and buy himself a pair of red suspenders.

"One day, my grandfather was having lunch in the grill downstairs in the Parker House. He sees that the president of the United States, Coolidge, is sitting at this table by himself eating Uneeda Biscuits smashed up in a bowl and covered with warm milk and some sugar. According to the bartender, this was his favorite, a real farm lunch. So my grandfather went up to him and said hello and Coolidge said something like, 'Shh, don't let them know I'm here.' "

"And nobody recognized him?" Josh says

"Well the bartender did and he said the Secret Service knew, but Coolidge didn't know that they knew and he thought he was putting one over on them. To me, the amazing thing is the most powerful man in the country could get on a train, go to Boston, buy suspenders, and almost nobody else noticed. Different era, I suppose."

"Why the red suspenders every time? Seems kind of weird," I say.

"You know how those Vermont farmers are, wild men, real Kraft-Ebbing time."

Paul starts the engine and we go back east. We stop at Caswell's and, seeing nothing, try to suck 'em up. Paul demonstrates his syncopated strip again.

"It's a tango," Tom says.

"What is?" I ask.

"The suck 'em up. Watch . . . *Dat, da dat, da dat dat dat.* You know 'Hernando's Hideaway' from *Damn Yankees*?" Without waiting for my answer Tom pulls himself up to his full, considerable height and, like a swivel-hipped lounge singer, he breaks into song:

> *I know a dark, secluded place*
> *A place where no one knows your face*
> *A glass of wine, a fast embrace*
> *It's called . . . Hernando's Hideaway*

"Fish the beats in this verse," he advises. "Strip hard on the accents."

Paul gives an unconvinced "Hmmm."

I'm game. Paul's strip, Tom's music. Josh and I cast out, let the fly sink and, with each of us singing the song, we begin to strip in line: strip **strip**, strip **strip**, strip **strip strip strip** . . .

"Okay, one thing," Tom says, "you know how everyone screws up the beginning of Beethoven's *Fifth*? They start right on the first powerful chord. But the song really starts on a rest. Same here, give it a slight rest, a hesitation, before you begin each set of strip strips."

Good point. That hesitation makes for a life-like rhythm instead of a by-the-numbers motion. I catch a fish. Josh catches a fish. Tom takes the rod and catches a fish. It's not an every-cast thing, but it surely ups our fish frequency.

"That is the strangest explanation of a flyfishing technique I have ever seen," Paul says, "but, hey, if it works . . . that's all that counts." Then, changing his tone to all business, he drops his voice and commands, "Okay don't react. Don't point. Just stay where you are. I see the beginning of something and I want to get there without drawing a crowd. So act like we don't have a clue that anything is happening and I'll just ease on out slowly, head way outside and then we are going to come down on a blitz."

Taking the long way around, Dixon succeeds in losing his usual camp followers and we come up on the Sewer Pipe where there are bass working. They porpoise ever so subtly, like trout. In the Rockies, in big lakes and back eddies, there is a phenomenon called "gulper fishing": big trout hanging in one place lazily gulping insects. The fish don't have to move much or make so much commotion because the insects are almost stationary. I would characterize the behavior we see now as the striper version of gulping. The surface betrays a hint of activity but remains, for the most part, unbroken. Under the white glare of an overcast sky, the activity is all but invisible to the birds. This explains why we have two hundred fish working and no birds over them.

It looks very trouty, very leisurely, more like the conditions Tom sees in the Adirondacks when the brown trout key in on emerging mayflies just under the surface. The ocean water looks pregnant; there is no other word for it. You know by looking at it that there is something underneath waiting to come out.

Tom steps to the bow, Josh has the stern. Taking their cue from the fish, they cast gently. A few days ago when stripers were slamming the boat in a blitz, we responded with equal energy and vigorous casts. In contrast, today, the subtle feeding that we have come upon calls forth delicate casts and equally smooth strips. The fish do their part, no violent strikes, just a slight but unmistakable tightening of the line. Paul backs the boat away from the pod. Josh and Tom subdue their fish, both keepers.

"Stay at it, guys," I say when they offer me the rod, "you've got the touch."

They each get a handful of fish. We are all alone. The ocean is quiet. The air doesn't move. The surf doesn't break, it laps the shore. We feel the serene, almost still-life quality of the setting. We don't say much. I take a turn, as does Paul. No double hauling, no distance casting.

I work on my cast, not because the situation requires it, but rather, since it doesn't, I feel no pressure to perform. I hear Paul's line whooshing through his guides. Mine sounds almost the same.

# October 16:
# The Littlest Bootlegger

≈

TOM LEFT AND TOOK the good weather with him. A nasty east wind piles seaweed on the rocks in front of my house. Gray, drizzly, no fun. I meet Vic Vecchio and Jens Lester at Mt. Fuji. Jens has his doubts about setting nets in this wind. We drive two miles to the beach to check things out and to see if it makes any sense to lug all the gear across the dunes to the haul seine beach.

Jens contemplates the surf. He gazes left, toward Napeague. It doesn't look horrid to me but Jens says, "Doesn't look too good for the dory. She doesn't do well with the ocean like this," referring to the way the tide runs east into the wind.

Walter tells a story of how he went out in an iffy sea once and ran into trouble.

"We were going to set that morning but the wind was blowing hard from the southeast. Richard, my uncle, was in the bow, I was midship and Harry was in the stern. The rest of the crews didn't set so they were going to help us push off because we were catching fish pretty good so we were going out there anyway (this was in the days when the boat was launched without a truck and it was rowed through the surf).

"So when we got a slatch [a break in a set of seas coming in] we tried to push off. Well, we only thought a slatch was coming, but it turned out it wasn't. So half of the pushers understood that we said 'Go' and the other half thought it was 'Ho.' We had three or four pushing and three or four holding, so we didn't get off too well. When we got in there we pitchpoled [turned a half somersault in the surf] and the boat went over. Richard and Harry dove over the side but I couldn't. So I grabbed the seat. The seas were banging the boat but I just stayed there (it would have been too dangerous to try and move with a mile of tangled net and lead weights shifting in the wash). In a situation like that you don't have much time to be scared: You get scared after you get out. It gets to you how close it was. . . . I was lucky to get out."

Since that day, Walter hasn't set a net.

Jens takes one last look at the sea and says, "Let's try tomorrow."

Before we all go our separate ways and make new plans for the day, we stand around and chat for a while. The guys are excited about the upcoming bow season for deer. I don't quite get it. Here we are in the midst of the greatest run in one of the world's greatest fisheries and Jens, Wally, Mitchell and company are all worked up over hunting pretty average deer.

On the other hand, if you spend all of your time around the water—with cold hands, wet clothes and salt-pickled skin—I can see the allure of sitting in a tree stand in the woods, waiting for a shot. The deer, fat on the berries and nuts of fall, will make an emphatic change from seafood, too. So I guess I do get the allure.

When we part, I drive across the bayside dunes to Napeague. There have been no reports of any action, but since I am out of the house already and have not checked that shore in a few weeks, it beats doing nothing at home. There are pound traps set at two-hundred-yard intervals along the pebbled shore. They are often full of bait, so it is possible that any bigger fish that haven't moved to the Point will come here to feed.

This stretch of beach begins at Water Fence, so called because in the days when Montauk was the common pasturage for the town's animals, a fence extended a hundred feet or so beyond the shore so that cattle could not wade around it. From my vantage point I can see birds between my house and Cartwright's; they're moving fast, but not albacore fast. Could be a school of blues, but too far away for surfcasting.

I am the only person within sight. A big sailboat rides on the horizon. From Napeague over to Accabonac and around Gardiners Island—which comprises the panorama in front of me—smugglers have found that a knowledge of shoals and reefs, inlets and coves, can assist the enterprising contrabander to evade the authorities' best efforts. Captain William Kidd, it is said, hid a treasure on Gardiners before he was apprehended, sent to England for trial and hung. Kidd, who had a letter of marque from the crown, authorizing his privateering, was justifiably upset with the court's ruling because he was playing within the rules: Nonetheless, he was hung for piracy.

More recently, during Prohibition, rum-running was a common occupation among the baymen of the East End. No one knew these waters like them: certainly not the Coast Guard nor the Treasury agents charged with keeping America sober. The torrent of liquor that poured into the United States from vessels coming from the north nearly "drank Canada dry," as the saying goes.

I have heard many tales of the derring-do of wily East End smugglers. For me the prize goes to Gus Pitts. The Pitts family arrived here with a group of Canadian seafarers brought to Montauk by the Anduin brothers, the owners of four boats that netted huge schools of menhaden. These fish were processed into meal at Promised Land, not far from where I had driven into Napeague. Gus's father worked there for seven years before he bought a dragger and went into business for himself netting fluke, sea bass, porgies, flounder . . . whatever was running. His young son had a feeling for the sea. He became an expert boat handler and navigator, which attracted the attention of the local rumrunners. Here is the story Gus told at a dinner with some of the other old timers at the Tipperary Lodge in Montauk in 1993:

"I worked with (i.e., was a rumrunner for) Phil Coffey. He used to give me half of a two-dollar bill. The captain of the boat where I picked up the rum had the other half. The first time I went out I found the place where the ship was supposed to be, but it had left. Instead of coming home for fifty-five miles from offshore, I looked for the boat. I eventually found it. I got the load but then my engine broke down on the way in. I was seven days out at sea before I got the engine fixed. I had to do it myself and I finally landed in Connecticut. When I landed, this guy gave me a cigar box to take home. He said, 'Give this to Phil Coffey.' This guy threw it in the front part of the boat. I didn't look in the box."

With his unopened cigar box, Pitts headed home, arriving at night. Because of the rocks all along the shore, Pitts was afraid of getting too close. Good seaman that he was, though, he had dead reckoned his ship quite near to where it was supposed to be.

"I anchored and swam ashore. Who did I meet but one of the guys I was working for?

"He said, 'Where the devil are you coming from?'

"I said, 'I was lost at sea.'

"He said, 'You were supposed to be here seven days ago.'

"I told him, 'The motor broke down and here I am.'

"They fed me and gave me a bed that night and enough gas to get back home. When I anchored the boat on the mooring, Joe Coffey (Phil's brother), comes to me and says, 'Did they give you a box to bring home?'

"I say, 'Yeah, it's in the boat.'

"Well, it turns out there's forty-five thousand dollars in that box!"

Young Pitts was thereafter judged to be resourceful, dogged and trustworthy. He was rewarded with the fastest boat on the East End:

"They got me an eighty-five-foot boat, with three Liberty five-hundred-horsepower engines. I was capable of making forty-five knots. On one run, I picked up a shipment from this big English yacht. I gave them the signal and they put me on side the boom. Their guy looked at me and said 'Where's the captain?'

"I said, 'I'm the captain.'

"He said, 'How old are you?'

"I said, 'Fifteen.'

"He says, 'Well, where's the mate? Bring him up here.'

"I say, 'The mate's eleven years old.'

"So they brought the two of us up before the captain. He was a big English about six foot six.

"The captain says, 'I've been at sea now for forty something years and I've never seen anything like this before. Two kids out here on an eighty-five-foot boot with three five-hundred-horsepower Liberties picking up five hundred cases of liquor!'

"They couldn't refuse it to me because I had the order. I put on five hundred cases. I got sighted by the Coast Guard just off of Fort Pond Bay here. So I started running. They chased me. I drew four and a half feet when the boat was filled, but when it was under way there was so much power, the boat rises up and we're only drawing two feet. I went over the shoal where they couldn't follow. I had three rowboats there with lights that knew just exactly where to go."

The whole shipment was unloaded and out of harm's way by the time the feds caught up with Gus.

I wonder if the pot smugglers of today will be looked on as loveable old rustics when my grandchildren come to Napeague.

# October 17:
## Portrait of An Artist

≋

12:05 A.M.: She is straight out of a Raymond Chandler novel, about five-foot-four, coffee-skin, shoulder length hair in long black waves, ankle-strap high heels and a scarlet dress slit just enough up the side to show you that the legs continue north in grand fashion. Her name is Brooke.

I am in the living room with my recently arrived guest, Al Caucci—the inventor of the revolutionary Comparadun series of dry flies and author of the modern troutfishing classic, *Hatches*. Caucci arrived about an hour ago. I poured us a glass of black scotch whiskey that Jacques sold me: I don't know how it gets this color, but it is quite smooth with lots of body. We are happy as clams, sitting in front of the fireplace. Up to this point, Al is impressed with my house, the view of the Bay and the defrosted leftover brisket. When Brooke shows up, I am sure that he thinks, for a moment, that he has died and gone to flyfisher's heaven.

That's as far as the Raymond Chandler fantasy goes, how-ever: Brooke is working on a television show that I signed on to write before I took this job, and she is delivering a tape that I need to look at so that I can write a few lines for a voice-over session. It is past midnight when she arrives and she hasn't eaten dinner. I serve her more of the endless brisket, show her the guest room and we all turn in.

In the morning we drive to Paul's—Al, Brooke and I. Paul has some new fly line for Al. Ernie French, who shares a house with Paul, has to drive to New York to deliver some cabinetry that he has built: One look at Brooke and he says, "No, not out of my way at all, glad to drive you wherever you are going."

Paul, meanwhile, has a large loop of flyline around his knee, another loop in his teeth and, with both hands, he twirls the line as he ties a Bimini Twist. With twenty-six twists, double loops, single loops and the requirement that it be seated just so, it may well be the Gordian knot that challenged Alexander the Great. It is a knot of great strength and I am not sure why Paul ties Al's line with it, but we are impressed. Al winds the new line on the reel and we are out the door by 7:30.

If it is true that as we age we begin to look like who we have become, Al, in his early sixties, looks like a professor in a Tuscan liberal arts college. He has a high receding hairline, dark mustaches and an erect, almost military, bearing. His professorship, if such existed, would be the Theory and Practice of Modern Flyfishing. This is not to say that "Cooch"—as he has been called by his neighbors since his roughneck childhood in a Philadelphia suburb—is a prim, school-teacherly type. He dresses in jeans, prefers Bob Dylan and John Prine to all other singers and drives a 1986 red Porsche—still a super hot car—with only 44,236 miles on it.

Al and I meet Levison at Diamond Cove shortly after 8:00. The wind blows at a steady 15 knots out of the east. Not terrible. In fact, it builds casting character, Al says, in the first of many soliloquies on the art of casting that he will deliver over the course of the next few days. Must be something in the Hamptons air, because just like Jim Clark and Sam Lester—in fact anyone on the East End over the age of fifty-five—he begins this monologue as if he is picking up a thought that has been under disussion. No matter that it comes out of the blue. He asks Jim to slow momentarily so that he can demonstrate while he lectures.

"People get freaked out about head winds," he begins. "It psychologically blows them away. But it shouldn't. Casting is all about a backcast (when the line rolls out behind you). A forward cast, even into a headwind, is just following through after your backcast loads the rod, flexing it, developing all of its power. If you think of it this way, you can load the rod much better with a twenty-knot wind in your face. Then, when you come forward, point the rod tip down and the line will go straight out. All you have to do is concentrate on bringing your forearm forward and rolling your wrist at the end. I'll show you exactly what I'm talking about. Jim, give me a nine o'clock shot into the wind."

Levison maneuvers the boat. Al strips out fifty feet of line. The wind comes straight at him. He pulls on the line with his free hand (beginning the double haul) as he flicks the rod backward. Caucci's style is more English, what I think of as old-fashioned. He stands straight keeping his elbow and forearm close to his torso (in the old books, the casting diagrams for beginners recommend that you put a book under your arm while you cast in order to keep your arm close to your body). Imagine a teacher pointing his finger and going tsk-tsk. Al's motion is something like that. When the backcast has unrolled, Al pulls again on the line with his free hand (timing is critical in this second part of the double haul) and, as he does so, he comes forward with his stroke.

Explaining the double haul is something that many fishing writers, myself included, have attempted. Nonetheless I doubt that anyone has ever learned how to double haul from reading a book. True mastery takes a lot of practice and observation of others. With perseverance, practice leads to an "Aha!" moment. Then, everything flows smoothly.

Andre Soltner, the gifted and hospitable chef who made Lutece *the* top restaurant in New York, had a test when someone came to apply for a cook's job in his kitchen. He didn't waste a lot of time on food theory. "Make me an omelet," he would say. That was all. The way a person makes an omelet would tell him everything about the way the newcomer handled food and dealt with heat. In like manner, if a caster can execute the double haul, you know he or she can master every other technique that flycasting requires.

Dealing with wind is the major challenge in all casting. We would all rather cast in tranquil air. But in the real world, at some point in the day, wind will often be your enemy. Where the average caster, trying to deal with a head wind, will attempt to muscle the cast and "throw" the line as if it were a baseball, this is not what Al does. Standing in the bow of Jim's boat, Al flexes the rod easily, comes forward and snaps his wrist downward, bringing the cast under the wind. Zoom. Out goes the line. Not a reel-clearing hundred-foot cast, but a respectable and accurate forty to fifty footer straight into the wind.

With the lesson completed, Al, like most newcomers at Montauk, is eager for an albie fix right away. But the albies are not in a mood to come up and stay up. We need to chase the fish, spin the boat, creep up on them and then take our shots quickly. Al is in mid cast, at the point of shifting his weight to come forward, when a rogue wave (not a monster bad guy, just a misbehaved youngster) catches us portside. My grandfather used to quote a Russian proverb, *"gavnoh y mahlo,"* literally "shit but not enough," which means if you come across a big pile of manure you will see it and walk around. A small pile of dog poo, however, is likely to go unnoticed until you step in it. The wave is *gavnoh y mahlo* and therefore a problem.

As the wave hits, Al's feet and legs go in the air, then Al disappears behind the center console of the boat. I hear a clunk—*his head?* Jim and I jump forward to make sure that Al hasn't tumbled overboard. We are relieved to see that he is still in the boat, but rubbing his head from a healthy knock: not serious, just enough to shake him up. "I'm fine, I'm fine," he assures us, so we continue along the rip looking for albies.

The waves continue. The fish are hard to come by and whether it is the aftereffects of the spill or plain old mal de mer, Al is a little queasy.

"Hey, no sense knocking yourself out on the first day," Jim says. "I don't think we are going to miss much if we call it quits now and save it for another day."

"Let's take a drive, Cooch," I suggest when we are back on shore. "I'll show you the lay of the land and the water. I have a special spot I think you'll like."

I turn onto a rutted, potholed road east of Napeague that Sam Lester has taken me down many times. We make our way through the forest, then tall grass, beach plums, wild roses and a maze of game trails. We descend through an opening in the bluffs to a pebble beach where the way is guarded from the casual angler by huge boulders and basketball-sized rocks that have eviscerated many transmissions.

To our right there is a long sweeping crescent stretching from Napeague east to Culloden Point. It was there, in a snowstorm on January 22, 1781, that H.M.S. *Culloden*, a 161-foot, 74-gun frigate—part of the huge British fleet deployed in Gardiners Bay—ran over the shoal at Shagwong before foundering on the rocks at Culloden. Somehow, the captain, George Balfour, was able to steer the crippled ship off the rocks and make it to the quiet of Fort Pond Bay where the ship sank. Miraculously, the entire crew of six hundred was saved.

The high bluffs make this spot inaccessible except to those who also know the route we have taken. The east wind that proved so troublesome off Shagwong is here blocked by Culloden so that the whole cove is flat water: good flycasting water. We take our rods from the Jeep and, for the hell of it, throw line as far as we can. I have on a popping bug. It makes an attractive burble on the surface of the water. If there is a fish around, it will come. Nothing happens, so we get back in the Jeep. Al and I have been at this game enough years that we feel no urge to force the issue.

"When I take people out on the Delaware River," he says, referring to clients that he guides out of his lodge in Starlight, PA, "I do like we're doing. I drive and I drive. If I don't see anything happening, I don't fish. My clients may or may not say anything but they always give me a look like, 'Man, I've spent all these hours out here and all he does is drive around and look—look at the sky, look at the water and sometimes dip his finger in the water.'

"Then finally it looks right and I say, 'Okay, let's put our waders on.' We go out there and still nothing's happening and he's looking at the water and he looks back at me, like, 'What are we doing here?' Then, all of a sudden you see the first rise and the second rise and then I say, 'Okay, here's the bug you better put on,' then badda-bing-badda-bang-badda-boom, in one hour we end up hooking fifteen, twenty fish between us. Then the guy says, 'What a day!' What he forgets is that we've checked all our options and they finally brought us to this spot. My point is one hour can make a fabulous day's fishing, but you have to wait for that hour and you have to be on the water then."

I toss in my corollary. "The difference between no fish and one fish is much greater than the difference between one fish and ten fish. In other words, if it gets to the last hour of the day and I haven't caught a thing, I am very dispirited. It's a zero day. If I catch one fish, one decent fish, then it goes in the file marked Successful Days."

I turn down a sandy track and we are at Hidden Lake, one of a string of natural freshwater ponds that run down the spine of the south fork of Long Island (basically, the Hamptons). As we walk from the Jeep, a family of swans paddles serenely away from us. The reeds have gone brown on top. A slicing V-shaped wake streaks in front of the reeds.

"Pickerel," Al says.

"Did you ever read Thoreau about brook-trout fishing in the freshwater ponds of Cape Cod?" I ask.

"No, why? Are there brook trout here?"

"Used to be, now these are bass ponds. Before I ever got into saltwater flyfishing I used to come out here with John Groth and we would fish these ponds in float tubes."

John Groth, first art director of *Esquire* magazine, now departed, invited me on my first fishing trip to the East End. John had a full head of snow-white hair and mustaches to match. A dapper gent. He was an artist in Chicago in the 1920s. As he told me the story, he was drawing pictures of the police beating up on some striking workers one day when Arnold Gingrich, the not-yet-famous editor and publisher, happened to pass by.

Gingrich had just inherited a magazine that was given out free to haberdashers. It was called *Esquire*. Flush with a small inheritance, Gingrich went to New York and stopped in at the Algonquin roundtable where he approached Hemingway, Benchley, Dorothy Parker and whoever else was in on the drinking party on that particular day. He offered each writer $500 for any unpublished work they had lying around. Even name-brand writers such as these had one or two rejected pieces in the file drawer, and five hundred bucks for doing nothing seemed like an agreeable offer.

Gingrich returned to the Midwest with almost enough editorial material, all by famous authors, to fill out the next edition of the new and improved *Esquire*. Eight more pages and he would have an issue. Groth's pictures, simple line drawings full of emotion, attracted Gingrich, who, Groth recalled, was pretty tapped out from his buying spree. "How would you like to be art director of *Esquire* magazine?" Gingrich asked Groth. Although John had never heard of *Esquire,* it was a job—something that was hard to come by in those years. "If you will let me run your drawings, the job is yours," Gingrich offered.

Groth accepted. He and Gingrich became close friends and associates and through Gingrich, John entered the world of fly-fishing. Gingrich went on to become a grandee of the sport and he founded the Theodore Gordon Flyfishers, an important fishing and conservation group. In many books and articles from the forties through the seventies, angling literature is full of the pictorial work of John Groth, although my favorite has nothing to do with angling: It is a heartwrenching illustrated version of Mark Twain's "The War Prayer," a blank verse poem on the perverse ironies of war where patriotic soldiers, mothers and children pray for death and destruction to be visited on the other side's equally prayerful, equally patriotic, soldiers, mothers and children.

On warm October afternoons, John and I took our float tubes down to the ponds near Sag Harbor. We would wade up, climb into our inner tubes—which were outfitted with a seat/harness—and move among reeds and lily pads, casting popping bugs for the largemouth bass with which these ponds had been seeded. John had no use for saltwater flyrodding. He wasn't physically up to it by the time I met him. But bobbing around in a protected bass pond in the middle of the forest was something he loved to do. He always wore a Greek fisherman's hat when he fished. As he moved across the pond, the smoke puffs from his corncob pipe produced the effect of a captain at the helm of very small tugboat in a children's book. We would stick a portable radio in one of the pockets of the float tube so that we could listen to the ball game (John was a Yankee fan). When he drifted too far away for me to hear the tiny speaker, I could tell how the Yanks were doing by his exhortations.

As I recall those days, I think that if I had my canoe along, I would give it a shot today. On second thought, I wouldn't. I am not interested in largemouth fishing now. I want one thing only this month. I am drunk on fishing the Black Hole, stripers on the Point. Although it's late by now, we take the Jeep down the track to Turtle Cove for a last look. With the Point framed by the trees along the dirt road, every move changes the relative positions of the moon and the lighthouse, in the way that buildings seem to move past one another when you walk across the piazza of a medieval city.

It is cold in Turtle Cove. Cornicelli and Levison are on the shore, watching the surfcasters. In the fierce rip, Blinken handles the waves in his sturdy boat. Bob Sullivan has a hell of a time in his flats skiff, but I have to hand it to him, at least he is out there.

Day One of Al's trip, plenty of exploring, pretty lousy fishing. If I had invited a part-time fisherman, I would have felt bad and had the urge to cheer him up. Cooch knows, though: Weather happens and you just wait it out and hope.

## October 18:
## The Story of the Stick Man

≋

A FRONT HAS SETTLED IN. The east wind rose 5 knots overnight and it's raining.

"Hey man, nothing you can do about the weather," Al says—a phrase, no doubt, that he has resorted to ten thousand times in his years as an outfitter.

Paul joins us for a drive to Montauk Harbor to check things out. Maybe the wind is coming in differently at the Point. Maybe the rain is holding off. Maybe we can get out in Paul's boat because his client has canceled.

One look at the entrance to the harbor and "maybe" becomes "not today."

Dixon and Al talk shop. Paul asks Al's advice about opening a lodge, a next logical step in building a real business on the East End. Al, who has owned his lodge on the Delaware for a number of years, advises caution. "It's a tough business and you have to look at the economics carefully. You can't price yourself out of the market."

Paul says "yup" in a way that I see that Al's assessment has registered. Paul drops us back at my house and returns home to play catch-up ball with his bills, his taxes, his laundry and all the other real-life chores that get put aside in the eat-fish-eat-phone-sleep cycle of the guide's day.

I tell Al about a guide who seriously bad-mouthed Paul in an anonymous letter about a year ago. A story appeared in a New York magazine that treated Paul like a star. The magazine received a letter, signed by a fictitious person, complaining about Paul's morals, sexual proclivities, drinking habits, seamanship, fishing acumen and, tellingly, his ability to attract the notice of the press. Paul read the letter and said it could only be one guy, a friend of mine, a former friend of his. I said impossible. I knew the guy well. It bothered the hell out of me. I called the suspect, mentioning the letter as I inquired into the rift between him and Paul. He knew nothing about nothing, said he had nothing against Paul, but in so doing he twice used the phrase "bizarre behavior." That same, rarely used phrase appeared in the letter.

I knew then and there what the score was. There was an awkward pause in our conversation. He knew I knew, but I didn't say it outright. I wish I had. The incident poisoned the air at the marinas for a while. But that is the nature of guiding. Everyone else is a horse's ass, their skill is nothing more than blind luck, their boats (as opposed to your boat) are unseaworthy, their rods suck. This lack of elan isn't universal, and hotheaded guides can just as quickly get chummy, but on fishless days, when motors break, when a client stiffs you on a tip, rancor rises.

Amanda catches flack because she's a "new boy," Blinken because he started with a bankroll, Levison because he's still learning, Ernie French because he's prickly and Paul because he is the rock star of the Point.

"When you get to a certain status in the business," Al says, "there are always going to be local guys who are jealous of you. Paul has great skills and taste. He is a thinker about flyfishing. He's well-traveled, well rounded, not just a fishing *mulyan* [American-Sicilian street slang for a "melon," a no-class person]. If there are local guys who are envious—and you can count on it that there will be—you just have to say, 'Screw it, that's their problem,' and move on. It took me a long time to figure that out."

Just then Dave Blinken calls. He has been canceled out today, too. Dave worked as a casting instructor for Al years ago and Al still has a soft spot for him. With the wind and the tide, Dave figures there is one place, just one place, that is fishable—at Accabonac, a stone's throw from my house.

This makes perfect angling sense—there being an unwritten, but commonly held credo that good fishing requires at least an hour and a half in the car. So after having driven a hundred and fifty miles over the course of the last two days, we end up five minutes from my house, if you drive slowly.

On the inside of the Neck, David says there is a drop-off no more than twenty feet from shore. The dune that faces Gardiners Bay—perhaps eight feet high—protects us from the wind. Here we are, three of us, with a collective seventy-five years of fly-fishing under our belts, fishing the same place that eight-year-old kids come to for snapper, blues.

I think I feel a bump. So does Al. We talk ourselves into feeling phantom fish. I am reminded of when I was nineteen years old, driving back to college from Spring Break in Florida. Rumor had it that dried banana peels, rolled in cigarette paper and then smoked, would get you high. We drove through Georgia and South Carolina with five banana skins in the boot of the car, right where the sun would beat down and dry them. They smelled like pungent tennis shoes. After some hours of this, when we couldn't bear the odor anymore, we rolled up a banana skin "joint" and started inhaling.

"Yeah, I think I am getting a buzz," someone said.

"Me, too, kind of mild, not superstrong, but *definitely* something."

"Do you think? Yeah, could be."

That's how Al and I were with every bump of our fly along the bottom and then, *mirabile dictu*, Al had a fish on. About a minute later, but not much more than that, he landed a young striper, about a pound and a half. A fishless day is now a one fish day—big difference.

Dave has to meet someone for dinner. Al and I stop in at the market and buy a swordfish steak. "Special recipe, I never make it anymore because of all the overharvesting but, hey, special occasion. Okay if I cook tonight?"

I'm game. I have known many chefs who are good fly tiers. The converse is often true as well. The skills are related. Flies are tied with organic material. Tying a grouse feather on a hook, for example, requires a feel for living things. Similarly, although you may follow recipes in a cookbook, they are not blueprints nor shop manuals. You can't tie flies the way you fix a carburetor. You need to feel your way through it. You have to feel your way through the ingredients and adjust to them in a way that isn't as cut and dried as assembling a carburetor. I tell you this because Al is, or was before he retired, a successful engineer. I have known as many good engineer cooks as I have known creative engineer flytiers—just Al.

Continuing the cooking thought, to really understand the making of good food a chef goes beyond the immediate task of chopping or mixing. He or she thinks about what happens where the surface of the food meets the heat. Will it crisp, steam, form a crust? Likewise a true flyfisherperson thinks not of the cast nor the rod nor the reel, but, rather, how does all of this preparatory activity affect the movement of the fly a hundred feet away? The subtleties of every pulse, every bump will attract or repel a fish. Al cooks well and I assist. Dicing up the red and yellow peppers, roasting off the swordfish chunks, melting down twenty anchovy filets in sambucca and combining them with sautéed fennel is a two-man job. Al's taste in music and mine coincide. John Prine sings one of his ironic songs of *le comédie humaine:* "Sally used to play with her hula hoops, now she tells her problems to therapy groups." It reminds us momentarily of our discussion of the psychology of fishing guides, but we are feeling too good about the world to go down that road again. We concentrate on the food.

Two glasses of wine finds us deep into food prep and end-of-day bonhomie. Al fills in the story of how a street kid from Bristol, PA, became an engineer who worked on the design of a particle accelerator for Einstein and then went on to become one of the most innovative American flyfishermen.

"In the late fifties, right next to my father's barbershop there was a famous gambling joint called the Wagon Wheel. Bristol was a no-mans land in terms of the mob. The Trenton mob had no jurisdiction and neither did the guys from Philadelphia. So this was a neutral area, a gangster DMZ. All of the local wise guys liked me because I was a football star. I played running back for Bristol High. I was also a straight-A student. I could have gone to college on scholarship but my family needed the money so I went to work as a laborer in a few factories and moonlighted as stick at the crap table (raking the dice). I'd be at the stick for twenty minutes, then twenty minutes at the peephole to check the incoming clientele, then twenty minutes off.

"This guy Frankie used to come in and say, 'What's a smart kid like you doing in a place like this?' He was the head of human relations and the union at an aircraft company. I told him that I was good at mechanical drawing and he told me that he would set me up with a job interview. So I go down and I'm interviewed and the guy says, 'Where's your resume?' Well, I don't have one. So I hear him say to his secretary, 'What the fuck's Frankie sending me now?'

"I came from a tough corner so I got right back in his face and said, 'Who the hell are you talking about? You can take your job and shove it up your ass.' So a couple weeks later Frankie comes in and asked how I made out. I told him and he says he wants to set me up with another interview at another place, Strouckoff Aircraft. I got that job. Even though I didn't have any experience, they trained me.

"At first I was doing details and drafting and then some design work. Then they sent me to school at night and they put me in the wing design department. I learned analytical geometry and stress analysis and I really got into it. I was going to school at night at Temple for engineering."

At around that time, Al married Betti the Beauty Queen (Miss 3M 1960) and began a family and his other lifelong love affair, fishing.

"There were no flyfishing magazines in those days and there were no flyfishing schools. So one day, I saw an ad in *Field & Stream* for this place that taught flyfishing in the middle of Maine. I called this guy, George, and he said, 'You come down here and I'll teach you right out on the lawn.' So we drove to Maine, four hours on a dirt road to the northern end of Baxter State Park. It took us two days to get there. George takes me out on the lawn and says, 'Go like this and go like that.' He casts a few times, then he says, 'It takes a long time to learn, keep practicing, see ya later.'

"I said, 'Wait a minute, what kind of flies do you use?'

"He said, 'We only use two kinds of flies here, over-sized Paramachene Belles and Hornberg Specials.' So Betti and I go out and it's a beautiful lake at sunset ten o'clock. I'm casting out and there are fish rising for hours on end and I can't hook one. I figure either I'm doing something wrong or George gave me the wrong flies. So I go to him and he says, 'You can't be impatient. You've got to stay with it. It takes a long time to become a flyfisherman.'

"I couldn't sleep that night. At six A.M. I tell Betti we've got to go, we've got to fish. She says, 'Oh no, why do we have to go fishing now?' but she already knows my answer. So we get in the boat and there's mist all over and we're putt-putting along and she yells, 'Watch out you're gonna hit a rock!' I veer off and a goddamned moose comes up with moss in his mouth.

"I pull into a cove and the fish are on top. We put the flies on and we're swishing and swashing and nothing's happening and I say, 'Dammit, there's something wrong here. Give me that box, Betti.' I throw all of the flies out and I scoop up some of the bugs that are on the surface of the lake. I hit the motor on and go racing back to the camp. I go to the office and I ring the bell. George comes out and says, 'I knew you were going to be a pain in the ass the first moment I saw you.'

"I said, 'George, these flies aren't working. I need different flies that look like these (the ones I scooped off the lake). He comes back with a cigar box full of gnarly old flies. I pick out a dozen and go out the door. The guy asks me where I am going and I tell him not to worry about it. I got back to the cove and bada-bing, I limited out in about a half-hour (there was no catch and release back then). I learned a big lesson, or better, I taught it to myself. If you don't look at what is on the surface, if you just willy-nilly put a fly on, you can go for days without catching anything. That approach led directly to my books with Bob Nastasi."

Their first book, *Comparahatch,* was followed by the classic and groundbreaking *Hatches* and three subsequent volumes. They were characterized by an exhaustive, highly detailed study of insect hatches and the feeding behavior of trout. The practical result was the Comparadun series of trout flies, a revolutionary simplification of fly tying: less flies, much more durable.

"When I wrote those books, I had a house full of aquariums with stream insects in them. In the field we would do countless seine tests on all the key trout rivers in America to see what bugs the trout ate and when. We also used my 'troutscope' [a Caucci-designed reverse periscope contraption]. Someday someone is going to have to do the same study with the fish out here and that's when the fishing is going to get a whole lot more sophisticated. Guys like Paul in the salt water and like Lee Wulff [one of the pioneers of modern American flyfishing] with trout and salmon—they are artists. Next there will be guys like me, scientists."

We sip our last sips. Levon Helm, the drummer and Arkansas-born vocalist of The Band, rasps out a version of Bruce Springsteen's "Atlantic City."

*Well they blew up the Chicken Man in Philly last night*
*And they blew up his house too*
*Down on the boardwalk they're ready for a fight*
*Gonna see what those racket boys can do*

"That's about the way it was," Al says.

# October 19:
# The Trout and Dan'l Webster

≈

OVERNIGHT, THE EAST WIND has come straight around with gusts to 26 knots out of the west. We meet at the Candy Kitchen in Bridgehampton to figure out what to do, given the weather: Me, Paul, Cooch, Amanda, Alex Powers and Mike Daunt, recently arrived from England.

When I first started fishing the East End I would come to the Candy Kitchen with Josh. At 4:30 or 5:00 in the morning, all the early fishing crowd would be there. In fact, the business was so dependable (and so depended on the Candy Kitchen being open) that the proprietors would show up after the trusted regulars had already opened the place, brought in the newspapers and started the coffee. We would serve ourselves and leave our money by the cash register.

Today, though, the place is long opened by the time we gather at 8:00. The air is filled with the aroma of crisping bacon, fried eggs and coffee. One portly fisherman in the next booth tells his buddies he was trolling live eels off the Point. "I caught four bass, all bigger than twenty-five pounds," he preens.

*Yeah, sure.*

It is maddening. Every one of us has been to the Point once

or twice a day. The fish are there, tearing into the bait. We have all seen the Black Hole right inside the curls of the big breakers. But there has been no reaching them. They are simply impossible to get to in the heavy seas in our small boats.

Vic Vecchio told me they have been pulling in good hauls off the beach at Napeague. That means some of the bass are on the move south and west so it should be worth a look. We caravan to Wainscott. Sure enough there are squadrons of gulls working over bait, but the sea is too rough for flyfishing.

I take care to avoid the soft, wet spots in the sand, or hogs, as the locals call them. Paul's wheel sinks in one of them. I have a board and a shovel for this situation. We dig and wedge the board under the tire. There must be something genetic about the inevitable Chinese fire drill that occurs with men in this situation—car stuck, guys pushing, driver alternating between forward and reverse: Everyone is compelled to yell out directions, often conflicting. Through much effort, or perhaps in spite of it, we get the car back on dry, firm footing.

Paul suggests we check in with Harvey Bennett. Harvey and Paul shoot the breeze for a while—two champion talkers going at it. They talk about boats, motors, the virtues and (considerable) shortfallings of the other guides and regulars. Twelve minutes into the conversation (I checked my watch), Paul asks, "So what do you hear from the beaches?"

This is the proper way to ask a fishing question: You lead up to it. If you are asking for the location of a particular hot spot a direct question is the trademark of an aggressive loudmouth who will spoil it for everyone else. You should always respond to a report of great fishing with something like, "You mean near the church?" or "The place that Sam Lester likes on the falling tide?" This indicates that you aren't pumping for virgin information.

Rule Number 2 is never follow up. If the first question doesn't yield a full answer, leave it at that. Then, with the next local that you approach throw in the information that you picked up from Conversation Number 1, such as, "I heard Sam Lester was doing well at his falling tide spot." This may elicit a reply like, "You mean by Waterfence or over at the old Navy road?"

Thus, by a bit of information here and information there, you vector in on the fishing hole. Sometimes this is more than a one day operation, but patience is the only way.

To Paul's question about how the fishing is going on the beaches, Harvey responds with a simple, "They are killing them. Lots of blitzes."

That is good enough for me to head to the beaches, but Paul is a boat fisherman and a Montauk Point one, to boot. So is Alex. So is Amanda. They take Harvey's reply to mean the fishing is good everywhere. Paul's boat can handle the seas, Amanda's can't. They invite Al and me, but Cooch has had enough of rough water and smaller boats. We beg off.

Shortly, Blinken calls. He suggests poling around Accabonac Harbor. "It's protected from the wind, the flats are beautiful and maybe we'll run into something. There is always a big fish or two that hangs out until the bitter end."

David keeps his flats boat behind The Springs General Store, so, once again, hours of driving bring us right in back of my house.

"Reminds me of the Bahamas," Al comments. "Twenty knots and you're driving everywhere, looking for a place to hide."

"In the spring, these white flats are full of stripers, big stripers," Dave says as he poles us along, looking like a Beach Boys version of a Venetian gondolier.

We pass an osprey nest. Dave points out its occupant, ahead of us, riding on the west wind. We are protected from the breeze at water level, but above the trees, Big Bird gets a nice boost from the moving air. Al takes up his position in the bow. He strips line, scanning the water as he does. We don't expect to see much. We are fishing only because we are going crazy from not fishing.

A bonacker rakes clams from the shallow water by the shore. A small commercial boat exits Accabonac Neck, probably on his way to check his nets in the bay. Squid are in strong, butterfish too. The bay is rough once you leave the protected waters of our harbor, but if he hugs the shore, it won't be a bad ride. From his vantage point, Dave can see over the low dune that separates the harbor from the bay.

"Gulls are working, big balls of them, moving fast. Looks like they are after bluefish. If the bluefish come in strong, that's when the bait start to move out, then the albacore, then the bass. It ain't over yet by a long shot, but things are moving along." Then, dropping his voice to golf announcer level, "Al, look at three o'clock about sixty feet, moving to twelve."

"Got it," Al says.

"That is a beautiful fish," Dave adds. "Not a care in the world and the whole flat to herself. I didn't really expect to see one today but sometimes you find a loner waiting until the last moment."

"That's what Vic said, too," I add. "The big ones know when it's time to go and they don't leave before that."

Dave is zeroed in on the fish. "Okay Al, I'm turning to give you an eleven o'clock shot. I don't want to get too close in this calm water. When you think you have it, take it."

Al stands straight and casts. He pulls hard on his double haul, lets fly, leading the fish by ten feet. He lets the fly sink.

"Now strip," Dave says.

Al gives the Clouser a gentle deliberate hop. We see the fly in the clear water. If we can see it, so can the fish. She swims past. If she were a bonefish, there would be no point in trying again. But stripers aren't always spooked by a second or third cast. Al offers the fly two more times with the same result.

Dave shrugs it off. "Hard to get them to eat on the flats this time of year."

My turn. Nothing moves on the white flat.

"They had brook trout out here?" Al asks, picking up on the comment I made yesterday when we were at the freshwater pond. Al likes salt water well enough, but in his angling heart he is a trout guy and I have intrigued him.

"They came up every freshwater stream in Long Island. I am sure we had them in the Gowanus Creek in Brooklyn. Did you know that Daniel Webster held the world record for brook trout for nearly seventy years for a thirteen-pound fish that he caught on the South Shore? About twenty miles west of here?"

Al half remembers. Dave is a virgin audience. So, while keeping an eye out for something to cast to, I share what I know of Daniel Webster and the Giant Trout.

The year was 1823. Webster was a passionate flyfisherman. He was so good at it that his rod had its own nickname, "Old Kill All" (this was before catch-and-release). When business brought him to New York, he often fished with Martin van Buren, originally an upstate boy who had risen through the ranks of local politics, and then national politics. Van Buren and Webster were members of a sporting club on what is now called the Connetquot River. There is a little confusion about this because a fellow named Sam Carman had a mill on the river and there is also a Carman's River further east. But it was the Connetquot. The mill is still there.

In the summer, like all trout and salmon, the brookies (which are technically char, not trout) would descend to the largest accessible body of water. For Connetquot trout that meant the Great South Bay which separates the mainland from the barrier beach at Fire Island. In the fall the sea-run fish returned to the Connetquot to spawn.

On a fall weekend in 1823, Webster and Van Buren arrived and were given a report of a huge trout feeding in the race below Carman's mill. It would have been a brook trout because the first brown trout did not arrive in America until 1883. Nor was the rainbow brought east of the Mississippi until 1874 by Robert Barnwell Roosevelt, the uncle (as well as fishing and hunting mentor) of Theodore Roosevelt.

The fishing buddies spent the better part of Saturday afternoon trying to entice the brookie, who could be seen feeding steadily, but he showed no interest in their flies. The next morning, before church, they left instructions with Van Buren's slave, Apaius Enos, to come get them if the trout went on the feed again.

In the middle of the sermon, the slave tiptoed into the church and gave the news. Webster and Van Buren tried to leave inconspicuously but the congregation knew the score so half of them trooped down to the mill with the anglers.

With Enos at the oars, the two anglers took Carman's rowboat into the mill pond. On Webster's second cast, the trout took. After a good fight, Webster led the trout into the landing net that Enos held alongside the boat. "We have you now, Sir!" the slave said in a phrase that has been memorialized in the title of a painting of the event.

The trout weighed in at over thirteen pounds on the mill scale. Webster and Van Buren went directly to their carriage and brought the huge brookie to New York for a dinner party where, according to legend, it was served at Delmonico's, New York's first temple of haute cuisine. The chef prepared it in white wine, showered with pan roasted almonds.

Some years ago, I went out to the Bellport Brookhaven historical society and looked through the records of the church that Van Buren attended. I also researched the local papers and the main sporting journal of the time, the *American Turf Register and Sporting Magazine*. There was no mention of the incident in contemporary records although a weathervane, said to be an enlarged copy of the fish, is part of the historical society's collection. For fifty years, it told the wind direction atop the steeple of the South Haven Presbyterian Church until it was struck by lightning and toppled in an incident that resulted in the death of a mule standing below. Delmonico's restaurant, by the way, didn't open until 1831, eight years after the trout was caught, but with legends, who's counting?

Historical glitches notwithstanding, the trout was recognized as the official world record. Furthermore, Stephen Vincent Benet wrote that Daniel Webster once out-lawyered Satan in a contest for a New Hampshire man's soul, so I suppose if anyone could have caught a thirteen-pound brook trout on Long Island, then Webster would have been a good candidate.

When I finish my tale, Al says, "As long as we are not catching fish, why don't we have a look at your cast, Bubbelah (his pet name for me)?"

By this time, I have internalized some of the casting advice and examples I have picked up: slow down, lead with the reel. I get off a nice cast.

"Once more," he says, like a doctor who thinks he has possibly heard something slightly off in his stethoscope.

I let go, again about seventy feet.

"Your stroke is good. You need more drift, though. I think the difference between a good caster and a great caster is one word, drift. You don't let your arm drift back far enough on the backcast and that starts a chain of events. If you don't drift back enough, you don't give the backcast enough time to load up the rod. So the result is you hurry your forward cast, but that doesn't really add any power at all. Go back further, then when the rod loads up, pull on the line (the double haul), come forward and drive that reel in front just like Sedotti told you. At the very end, and only at the end of the cast, roll your wrist. This will give you a tight loop that punches into the wind.

"As the line shoots, never let it fall from your free hand. You want to make sure you have taken up all the slack by the time the fly hits the water. Now, here's the big difference from trout fishing. On a trout stream you stop the rod at eleven o'clock rather than rolling the wrist like I just told you. Why? Because, in the river, you want to develop slack so that, as the current takes the slack out of the line, the fly floats naturally without any drag. It's different in salt water especially when fishing the flats: You need to cast a straight tight line and start the retrieve immediately as the fly hits the water so that you completely *eliminate* the slack. Rolling the wrist, following through with the rod tip is the only difference between the end of the fresh- and saltwater cast . . . but it's a big difference."

*Drift. Haul. Don't let go of the line. Drive with the reel. Roll the wrist. Take up the slack.* I pretty much get it all except that my double haul, which I have been doing my whole life, falls to pieces.

"Don't worry about the haul," Al says. "Your stroke is very strong and you can get by without it. Your double haul will come back."

I sure hope so. I have always taken pride in my double haul. When you do it correctly the line shoots forward and slaps against the reel at the end of the cast. This tells you that you have developed power to spare. You know you have nailed it. Still, I am determined to work on these new (to me) refinements. I cast behind a large rock, right where Dave directs me. A spray of bait leaps from the water.

"All that bait and no fish," he says. "I think that we are not going to find any stripers."

We call it a day. It is killing me that we know the bass are in at the Point, that any day now they may start to leave and we can't get to them.

# October 20: The Saltbankers

≈

SOME PEOPLE ARE BORN HAPPY. Wally Johnsen is one of them: easy to be around, with a bushy beard and a wide smile, he would look right at home in a Frans Hals scene, where I am sure he would make friends with a whole tavern of Dutchmen.

Of all the boats in the flyrod fleet, Wally's boat, the *Mischief*, is the least sleek but most seaworthy. At twenty-seven feet (actually twenty-six feet, eleven inches, which keeps it in the small boat class), it is powered by an inboard Chrysler 460 cu engine: As Wally puts it, a "marinized version of a Ford engine block of the 1970s, before the gas crunch when cars were fast and engines were big." It is the boat I want for Al on his last day: It can handle just about any seas.

The morning breaks clear with a northwest wind. Nothing major but enough to freshen the air with autumn. Al and I stop in at The Springs store. Breakfast is a BLT on a roll with a scrambled egg, mayo and ketchup. Not a very complicated dish but, for some reason, usually confusing to order. If you ask for a scrambled egg on a roll with bacon, lettuce and tomato, for some reason, 90 percent of the short-order cooks in the world hear this as a bedevilingly intricate recipe—perhaps eaten only in Finland by effete aristocrats. Don't ask me why this is so, but it is. If, on the other hand, you say as I have learned to, "BLT with a scrambled egg and mayo," that's what you will get. Deal with the ketchup on your own or the order will go off the tracks again.

Wally waits at the slip at the Crabby Cowboy, his Chrysler engine burbling powerfully. He casts off the lines and we are under way within minutes. Before we get around to asking him, he tells the story of the boat. It's the first question people have, because the *Mischief* is the only one of its type in the flyrod fleet.

"It was built for tuna guides for long runs out to the Hudson Canyon. The guys who commissioned it ran out of money and it just sat there for six years before I bought it six years ago. It can fish Montauk when nothing else can," he says more from paternal pride than adolescent boastfulness.

Paul hails us on the radio: "Spider crabs, lots of them, but we can't get the stripers to eat." This is par for the course with these tiny crabs. They disperse over a large area instead of con-solidating the way that rainbait or herring will. Paul hasn't been into a blitz for a few days. Nobody has. Between the weather and the vagaries of the migration, the albacore have slowed, the blues have begun to show in greater numbers, and bass have yet to reappear.

A number of the flyrodders work under a line of birds.

"Big blitz," I say hopefully.

"Whatever is happening, it is more spread out than you think," Wally cautions. "When you see people under birds, I don't know if it is an optical effect or wishful thinking but it gets foreshortened, like looking through a telescopic lens."

"You want it to be a big blitz, so that's the way you see it?" I reason.

Wally pushes down the throttle. "Something like that. Anyway, there's action there, so let's go look."

"Big bluefish, really big," Jim Levison says as we pull up. "Hard to catch, though. They're eating small bait and they aren't boiling on the surface."

Further on I see Amanda, Ernie and Dave Blinken. Nobody has a rod bent in combat. Still, this looks like the only game in town, so we join the crowd.

"I see a slick in back of us. Must be something under them," Wally says and backs down fifty yards. For the first time since I have begun my fishing pilgrimage I am able to see a slick. It is a subtly shiny patch of water—actually fish oil—that rises to the surface when game fish chew their way through concentrated bait. Fish oil on top means feeding fish below. The slick will have drifted with the tide so Wally adjusts our position.

I cast a sinking line ahead of the slick and count to 10-Mississippi before I begin my strip. Instantly I come tight to a violent pull. The rod bends quickly, the line sizzles through the guides. Christ, it feels good to have a fish on again! And then it is off.

"Bluefish," Wally says.

That is all the action we see for a while. David has lent us a new hi-tech rod that he has been asked to check out. Al casts it then hands it to me. "Try it and tell me what you think."

I remember Al's instructions and his recent lecture on drift but it doesn't do me much good. Or maybe it's the rod. "Feels soft, Al," I say.

"It's like linguine," he agrees. "Now try mine."

I take up Al's Loomis. It feels as light as the rod I have just cast but it develops greater power.

"It gets me crazy if the gear isn't perfect," Al says. He is a mandarin about equipment: rods, flies, lines, knots—they all have to be just so. "After age fifty it's all about equipment; makes fishing less work. I'm for less work."

It's midafternoon. There is nothing to do but talk and cast. We move over to the north side, just west of Stepping Stones. We drift back to the Point. The flat has the green water, white sand, and windblown look of a tarpon flat in May when everything has shut off for a few hours. That's the time to "stake out," plant your push pole in the sand, and wait for the fish to come through. While that may work in the Florida Keys, the bottom and the currents at Montauk don't allow for this maneuver. We could anchor, but I have never done so. Flyfishing is active, even when there is no activity. You keep moving, keep looking.

We try the Tango Strip—Paul's syncopated sinking retrieve. A few fish respond. Not a blitz, but just enough activity to keep us from falling asleep, which would be easy in the soft, warm sunlight and the rocking seas. The fog horn at the lighthouse sounds like a snoring cow.

It's a good time for a sea story and Captain Wally obliges with the tale of the *Gertrude L. Thebaud*. "My grandfather was Knut Johnsen," he begins, "a great sailor. Everyone called him Charley, I guess because Knut was such a foreign name. He knew how to handle boats and was often called on by Jay Culhane who later owned Cutty Sark liquor. They would go off Newfoundland—supposedly 'fishing.'"

As Wally's uncle, Canny, once told me, "You had to catch some fish some time or the Coast Guard would catch you." On these putative fishing trips, Charley would put in at St. Pierre and Miquelon, the French islands off Canada, where they would load up with liquor. Charley Johnsen gained a reputation as a man who knew the waters from Newfoundland down to Sag Harbor, around Montauk Point and on into Brooklyn.

In 1920, William H. Dennis, the publisher of the *Halifax Herald*, put up the $4,000 purse for a trophy race among fishing vessels that worked the Salt Banks (the codfish grounds of the Grand Banks). Sailing ships had traditionally played an important role in the local economy. Working out of Nova Scotia ports, huge schooners would fish off the Banks for cod, which they salted and preserved at sea. The Canadians shared the fishing grounds with somewhat trimmer vessels from Gloucester, Massachusetts, that often loaded up on fresh fish and then sped to port. Salted or fresh, first to market meant higher prices so speed was important.

The rival Nova Scotians and Gloucestermen agreed that the sailing yachts that competed in the America's Cup (started in 1851) were not "real" ships. These gaff-rigged racing schooners carried enormous amounts of canvas, upward of 16,000 square feet on a single mast that sometimes reached heights of 175 feet (on a vessel less than 150 feet in length). They were built to catch the wind but not too much of it. If the wind speed went above 20 knots races were often canceled.

The Saltbankers, who were used to working in winter gales of 30 to 40 knots, thought that these toys of the yachting class were milquetoast abominations. In response to this general feeling, William H. Dennis endowed the International Fisherman's Trophy as the prize in a competition among true working fishing vessels—craft that could handle any weather and any seas—very unlike the high-strung thoroughbred boats of Newport.

The first race was won by the American *Esperanto,* a feat that President Coolidge called "a triumph of Americanism." Good old Calvin, pridefully vaunting America's twentieth-century superiority in the antiquated technology of sailing ships. The Canadians took this as a challenge to their national manhood. They commissioned the construction of the ship *Bluenose*—a fishing vessel, but one especially designed to win races (its likeness appears on the Canadian dime).

The Canadians gained the prize in 1921 and never relinquished it as the series continued, by fits and starts, until 1938. The captain of the *Bluenose,* Angus Walters, was well known as a skilled but nasty competitor. One after another, the American vessels that were built to take on the *Bluenose* proved not to be up to the job.

With the building of the *Gertrude L. Thebaud* (named after a New Jersey–born summer resident of Gloucester who bankrolled the boat), the Americans had high hopes that the *Bluenose* would finally meet her match. What's more they had the talented Captain Ben Pine, a Newfoundland man by birth, but a Gloucesterman since age ten. In 1923 Pine came close to beating the *Bluenose* at the helm of the *Columbia,* which he called "the finest piece of wood ever." Records of the race show that he had, in fact, crossed the finish line first, but Angus Walters claimed a technical infraction of the rules. The possibly partisan masters of the race—i.e., the representatives of the *Halifax Herald*—ruled in favor of the *Bluenose* and the hard feelings put an end to the International Fisherman's Trophy for eight years.

In 1930, the year of the christening of the *Gertrude L. Thebaud,* Sir Thomas Lipton (as in Lipton tea) was best known in sailing circles as the sponsor of four unsuccessful tries for the America's Cup. He put up the purse for a new competition of the Saltbankers. It was to be a rematch of the bitter rivals of 1923, Walters vs. Ben Pine.

Two days before the grudge match, Pine came down with appendicitis. The Americans needed a captain. Knut "Charley"

Johnsen, rumrunner/yacht racer/fisherman and grandfather of Wally Johnsen, stepped in. The race was neck-and-neck from beginning to end. As the Gloucester newspaper reported:

> With (the Thebaud's) better fitting sails and a tremendous superiority in windward work, the Nova Scotia Queen never had a chance. In three thrashes by the wind, the Thebaud picked up the most of her big lead. In the first round the Thebaud covered the six miles in 29 minutes and 3 seconds at a rate of about 12.35 knots per hour. The Bluenose, showing her fastest sailing on that third leg, first round, was only a second faster than the Gertrude in 29 minutes and two seconds.
>
> There was no mercy on the sea, the long, rolling swell, accumulation of several days of easterly wind giving the boats a tossing from the start to finish. They plowed through it like majors, one minute they were hull down and then re-appearing as they rode the crest. The Thebaud's Captain out jockeyed the Bluenose at the start and the minute and 15 seconds he secured over his adversary was enough open water to bring him a victory.

Angus Walters lost the race but refused to concede that his boat had been bested, claiming that a careless tactical decision on the stretch run cost him the lead.

Johnsen returned home a national hero. The boat and crew were even sent to the Chicago World's Fair in 1933.

"What happened to him after he finished being famous?" I ask Wally.

"He fished on his boat, a dragger called, the *Ruth Mildred.*

He also sold ice to commercial fishermen. After Prohibition, he bought the ice from Ballantine, the same company that made the beer. They had refrigeration equipment which produced more ice than they needed. The ice was off-loaded onto our Model A flatbed truck and they drove it down the dock to the ice chipper. One day, while getting ice to the chipper, a 'rocker'—a three-hundred-pound block with a chip that made it unstable—fell off the truck and hit Charley. It killed him right there."

"He got his start rum-running, and then was done in by ice from a beer company. Full circle," Al says.

"And the ship?" I ask, "the *Thebaud*?"

"Went down in a storm in Venezuela in the forties. Most of them went down in storms or wrecks," Wally answers.

Not most, all. The Saltbankers were ships built to take almost anything the sea could throw at them, but the final round always went to the ocean. None died "a natural death" in the salvage yard. According to Courney Ellis Peckham, the historian at the Essex Maine Shipbuilding Museum, the *Esperanto,* winner of the first race, went down on Sable Island in 1921. The *Elsie* sprung a leak and was lost off St. Pierre. The *Henry Ford* foundered off Martin Point, Newfoundland. The *Columbia* blew apart while haddock fishing on the Grand Banks in a hurricane. The haughty *Bluenose* "died on Caribbean reef in 1946" and the *Thebaud,* reduced to running small freight loads off Venezuela, sunk there in 1948.

By the time Wally finishes his sea story we have moved half-way to the lighthouse. Dixon, on a parallel and equally unproductive drift, points at schools of bluefish in the distance. At least that's what they look like judging from the activity of the birds. "When the blues show up like this, The Run is usually past its peak," Paul says, echoing Blinken's comment of the day before.

He could be right, but, on the other hand, he is off to Harkers Island, North Carolina, for three weeks to chase albacore twice the size of the Montauk fish. Since he is the one who often advises clients, "You don't leave fish to find fish," I'm hoping Paul is just saying this so that he doesn't look like a feckless angler—but Paul is usually right. The Run may not be over, but it is not getting bigger by the day anymore either.

Blinken pulls up. "Beautiful day. Should be perfect, but I don't like it. The fish are acting weird." Then, as if someone had fired off a shotgun, he barks, "My God! Look at that!"

First a hundred, then a thousand, then two thousand gulls come screaming down at the water. With no other warning, the bass explode fifty yards in front of us: furious, foaming, churning, sounding like a combine going through wheat. Paul, Wally and Dave start their engines simultaneously. We sprint to the Black Hole, but as soon as we get there it's gone. The birds fly off like looters caught in the act, affecting an "I'm just out for walk, doing nothing" kind of look.

"If they were here, then they are still here," Wally says. "They've probably gone down. Let's dredge."

I take three bass with my newly perfected (that is, newly perfected for me) Tango Strip. Above us the scattered birds reassemble. They swoop and rise, circle, dive, and circle again. There is an air of expectancy. The birds look, we look. We are down to Al's last shot. We wait.

"Jesus!" Wally half shouts, half whispers, "they're right in back of us!"

Western light, shafts of gold piercing the jade green water, then the dark trembling cloud in the depths: rising to the surface, brown-turning-to-red, an arc of leaping baitfish and then, with a whoosh, the glistening black backs of bass. Their banging against the sides of the boat beats a loud tattoo.

Cooch, who ten seconds ago gave the impression of a man about to fall into deep sleep, leaps up. He doesn't bother to false cast. He simply lets off one backcast, comes forward, drops the fly, strips and—Bam!—he is into a fish. I let go of the fly on my backcast, turn and strip twice. I feel the jolt that I have missed during these last few windy days.

With both of us hooked up, we fight our fish; or maybe it would be more accurate to say they lead us on a dance around the boat. Al completes a circuit. I lift my rod and allow him to pass. He reverses and comes back. Now my fish sends my rod over Al's as he dips for me in our flyfishing gavotte. We are fighting two animals that want to live and this is the way they burst for freedom. I land my striper, Wally leans over and unhooks Al's. Both nice fish, keeper size.

Al gets his fly back in the water. I do the same. We hook up two more times in this adrenaline rush of Mother Nature. The blitz, a vortex of entropy, lasts ten minutes, every one of them great. Then it shuts off. Just ten minutes after the whole week, but that's enough.

"Now I get it, this Montauk thing," Al says with a blissed-out beatified look. It doesn't matter to him or to me that we spent four days for those ten minutes. There is no equation to balance here other than the fact that time on the water will, at some point, equal good fishing. We put in the time, we got the fishing. I am glad that Al is enough of an angler to have waited it out. Sometimes it takes that long. Sometimes it doesn't happen at all. If you fish, you know this. Al leaves happy.

# October 21:
# Dead in the Water

≋

THE PLAN FOR THE DAY was to sleep in and mess around with the kids, go for a bike ride, drive the beaches. But since I am wide awake at 5:00, Alex Power's invitation to fish with him launches me out of bed. I should have known that when I went to sleep; fishing always wakes me up as faithfully as the muezzin calling the believers to prayer.

Now that Cooch has seen a Montauk blitz, our angling community has turned its efforts to securing one for Alex's fishing partner, Michael Daunt, the Englishman with whom we break-fasted at the Candy Kitchen. Daunt, an exuberant bon vivant, is a popular reciter of poetry in his homeland, a good amateur cook and the man generally regarded as the top Spey casting instructor in the U.K.—which would therefore make him tops in the world. In his mid-fifties, with a monk's tonsure, bright red fishing scarf and Barbour coat, he is the picture of a modern English sportin' gent.

Where the American double haul is wide open and unre-strained, using the whole body and extending the arms, the Spey cast is its equally exuberant English counterpart. Both casts are designed for distance. The difference with the Spey cast is that the angler holds the rod with two hands and roll casts the line forward, rather than backcasting and forward casting. A Spey-caster on a skiff in a rocking sea calls up the image of a cowpoke holding on to his lariat with two hands as he tries to bring a lassoed calf under control.

We are the first boat on the water today. We chase a few birds, but there are no blues, no albies, no bass . . . no blitzes. We attempt to circle the Point but the west wind and the south-east swells look ugly. Tommy Cornicelli radios us that there are blues working at Shagwong. If it's to be blues or nothing, we vote for blues. Daunt is enthusiastic. "Bloody mahvelous," he says. Everything about Montauk is marvelous to him—the free and easy flyrod scene, the towering cliffs, the rips, the birds. I suppose if I had never seen a blitz I might share his feeling right now, but truly "mahvelous" calls for a blitz, anything else is just a nice day on the water.

We chase blues back and forth over Shagwong rip. People often say that blues are easy to catch, and indeed they can be. But it is not a given. We have blues in front of us, in back, on either side, but they don't take. There is not enough bait schooled up to make the blues fearless and unmindful of the boat traffic. We cast anyway, pick up, move and cast again.

"Hmm, motor sounds funky," Alex observes. He checks the engine and finds the oil level is low: This can wreck an engine. He doesn't want to risk running in and ripping up the moving parts. Luckily, considering our lack of it thus far, we are in one of the few places near Montauk Point where phones get rea-sonable reception. I know Paul is taking Josh out today. Maybe they got a late start.

They did. They will bring oil for us. We wait, drifting. The wind hums along at a good pace. We are not in danger but the rising wind and opposing tide on Shagwong Reef—scene of so many wrecks—occasions a morbid thought or two, but mostly we chat about the things that interest us. For instance, poetry. Michael is a fan of Yeats and Emily Dickinson. I feel the same way. As we drift, he recites for us from Yeats:

*Why should not old men be mad?*
*Some have known a likely lad*
*That had a sound fly-fisher's wrist*
*Turn to a drunken journalist;*

"Present company excepted," he finishes.

"If you say so," I answer, "though in my dark hours, Yeats seems right on the money."

I ask Mike to demonstrate the Spey cast. Our American rods are not the ideal instruments for it, but in a boat, without a motor, five miles from port, they are all we have so they will have to do. Anyway, the rod isn't everything. I have seen Joan Salvato Wulff, a prodigious caster, cast forty feet of line in a tight loop . . . without a rod!

Daunt sits as he demonstrates. He talks and casts effortlessly. "The Spey cast is very much like a roll cast," he begins, referring to a commonly used casting tactic among all flyfishermen. To visualize a roll cast, imagine a lariat loop perpendicular to the ground, or a hula hoop rolling along. The roll cast uses the friction of the line against the water to flex the rod and propel the line.

"The Spey cast was developed, of course, on the Spey River," he continues, "because when you are down at river level, casting to salmon, the cliffs rise up in back of you. There is no way to backcast so the Spey cast is executed, thus"—he lets go a roll cast and redirects it in mid-motion—"it was the only way to get line out, an invention of necessity. A good caster—not a miraculous one, mind you, but a good one—can shoot one-hundred-twenty feet of line much more easily than with the conventional rod. The problem, however, is that your arms get tired with the big heavy rods. It's easier to cast all day with the American rod."

As the lecture concludes, Paul pulls up, bearing a plastic container of oil. Alex takes the cover off the engine. I hold on to Alex's belt loop to keep him from pitching over into the building seas. Salt water splashes on the engine while we have the cover off. Alex finally gets the oil in, closes the hood and starts her up. Sounds okay to me.

Not to Alex. "We're probably fine, but with salt water in the engine you never know. I think the smartest thing is to make our way in."

To escape the wind on our return, we duck into the semi-protection of Oyster Pond, just east of Shagwong. There are birds looking interested and maybe a boil or two. We cast. We catch nothing.

"Enough playing around, let's go," Alex says.

They drop me at the dock. The engine sounds fine the whole way in, so they can go back out if they want. The wind grows more wicked by the moment, but Daunt wants his blitz and, even more, Alex wants to get him into one. I have had my morning's fishing, such as it was, and my family is due at the station for the balance of the weekend.

In the evening, Paul, who plans to leave for Harkers Island and the Outer Banks on Monday, throws a farewell party: lobster, champagne, lots of white wine. Daunt arrives shortly after us with the aura of a man who has just arrived from a life transforming audience with the Dalai Lama.

"We stayed out late, the wind got rather nasty, but I finally got my bass blitz. Quite wonderful. I see what you mean now about those blitzes."

This tickles me. Here we are—me a mongrel Russian Jew/Polish Catholic, and Mike a veddy English Englishman—using the word "blitz," a term with infelicitous connotations for our peoples, to describe something we deeply enjoy.

Mike, like me, is one of those guys who naturally joins the kitchen detail, so we set about disjointing and cracking the cooked lobsters to drain most of their water before serving them up. It is a sloppy job that we embrace with messy gusto. Sending up explosions of flying lobster shards and drenching oneself in the inevitable squirts and splurts that follow seems of a piece with the excess of the bass blitzes: You cannot crowd more living into a moment than we are now.

Scott Holder, a very likeable guide with whom I haven't had more than the opportunity to trade "great fishin', huh?" pleasantries on the water, talks about his just-arrived boat the way other men dreamily tell you they have finally won the heart of an exceedingly beautiful and rich woman.

Paul has invited Blinken, a welcome gesture of hatchet burying. Amanda, friends with both, is delighted. Her natural social buoyancy becomes positively effervescent. Her laugh rises above the Rolling Stones playing loud on the stereo.

Lily and I sneak off to watch the World Series. She sits on my lap in the darkened room that is piled high with fly-tying material, vises, hooks, fishing books, fishing magazines. It's the Subway Series of 2000, Yankees-Mets. I have waited forty-odd years for this repeat of the interborough rivalries of my childhood. Somehow, though, as with everything else except that which happens off the tip of Long Island, I haven't paid much attention to it. The fishing, the fishing, the fishing; it's all there is.

Paul announces the showing of a private "porno flick"; i.e., a fishing video of a day's tarpon fishing in the Florida Keys. "Well all right," is the general feeling in the air, "we have fished every day for four or five months, fished in cold and wind, fished through clients as cheery as Himmler. So if you are showing a fishing video, then that is exactly what we want to see when we have some time off with our friends." Really, no irony.

So we gather in Paul's bedroom. His two sons—Austin and Andrew—climb around, under and through the legs of the adults in the packed room. We crowd the bed and floor. Peter Smith Johannsen, the youngest guide in the flyrod fleet, Alex, Michael Daunt, Scott, David, Amanda.

Paul rolls the tape. A sunny May day in the Florida Keys. A man stands on the front of Paul's skiff. He casts like a pro. The water is clear, green over a white bottom, like Caswell's on a calm sunny day.

"Okay, I think we have a school, a really big school coming at us about one hundred yards off," Paul advises the angler. "Holy Christ. Here they come!"

We see the dark shapes in the water, at this distance they are an undifferentiated mass. Paul continues to direct. "Lead them, straight in front. Take your shot."

The angler gets off a monster cast, one hundred twenty feet. We can make out individual shapes of tarpon now in the pod. They are five, six feet long, three hundred fish. You can pole the flats for a year and not see a pod that big. We gasp at the fish, we gasp at the cast. A tarpon turns.

"Strip, strip, strip," Paul counsels sotto voce. Then, still quietly but with mounting excitement, "Okay, he has it! Come tight and lay it into him."

The tarpon erupts from the water and our voices fill the bedroom with admiring oaths.

The tape cuts to the same setting, later in the action. Paul narrates: "Okay, the fish is about two hundred yards out and he has hung the line up on some coral under our boat. So I have to do my fearless guide thing."

In the video, Paul takes off his hat, his shirt, his glasses, hands his wallet to the second angler in the boat and dives into the water. He swims underneath the boat and frees the line. The huge tarpon sprints off on another leaping, head-shaking, tail-walking run.

Cut to: an hour and twenty minutes from hook-up. The tarpon, exhausted (but no more so than the angler), lays on his side next to the boat. Paul pushes it into the boat. They weigh it—165 pounds. Then they release it, but the tarpon is so spent from the fight that it just lays there, not moving.

The triumphant angler, having just seen Paul dive in the water like Johnny Weismuller in a Tarzan movie, goes in after the tarpon to grab it and revive it. Apparently, he thinks this is what cool guys in the Keys do.

"No, no, no," Paul screams emphatically. "For Christ sake, get back in the boat! Now!"

But he is intent on reviving the tarpon. He takes hold of it and moves it back and forth in the water to force water through its gills. The maneuver works and the giant fish swims away.

Paul explains why he yelled. "When the fish was two hundred yards out, if there was a hammerhead following it, I was safe. But if that hammerhead had followed the tarpon in . . . not pretty. That guy was lucky he wasn't chopped in half."

A shark once attacked a tarpon that I was fighting off the Marquesas in the Keys. It looked like an explosion in the water and then my line went slack. Pretty scary, even at a distance.

When the video is done, we are spent, like the audience leaving a well-done action film, say, *The Road Warrior.*

Fishermen, getting together to talk about fish, look at pictures of fish, watch a movie of fish. Finally, it is time to break up the party because we all have to get up in the morning . . . to fish.

# October 22:
# Truth and Radio

≋

WHEN MY FATHER WAS a young boy, twelve to be exact, he was sitting in the kitchen of his parents' apartment in Washington Heights, overlooking the recently completed George Washington Bridge. Their guest that night, as she was many evenings, was Celia Weiner, a sweet dumpling of a woman whose cheery exterior hid the missionary soul of a fire breathing Marxist. My grandma, also named Celia, served dinner. She meant well in the kitchen but she regularly turned out a pot roast so dry that it could desiccate a rain forest. A mound of pressure-cooked mashed potatoes accompanied the beef.

Shortly after 8:00—it was a Sunday night—the radio broadcast was interrupted for what sounded like an on-the-scene news report from Grover's Mill, New Jersey. Martian invaders had landed and were cutting a path of total annihilation on their way to New York. The family was listening, although they didn't know it, to Orson Welles' famous Halloween docudrama, an updated version of H. G. Wells' *The War of the Worlds*.

My father was terrified. When the report came of the George Washington Bridge being engulfed in an inferno of Martian flames, he remembers screaming, "Mom and Dad, we have to leave now! The Martians are coming!"

Celia Weiner didn't believe one word about Martians. She was sure it was an Axis sneak attack on the Upper West Side. "Never mind Martians," she said, fortifying herself for the barricades with a huge mouthful of potatoes, "it's the fascists."

Had they believed their eyes more than the media that filled their ears (and their imaginations) all the dinner group had to do was look out the window at the George Washington Bridge over which traffic moved smoothly, unobstructed by Martian war vehicles.

I think of this family legend shortly after I wake up this morning. What leads to this Proustian moment is that the Irish Robot says it will be a nice warm day with light winds out of the northeast 7 to 14. I look forward to accepting Dave Blinken's invitation to take my family on a tour of Gardiners Bay and the Point. We will even put a few spinning rods on board so that Lily and Melinda can catch fish if we come upon a blitz. The phone rings. It's David. "Sorry man, I guess it's a blowout."

"What do you mean, they said northeast seven to fourteen."

"What are you talking about? It is howling a ton out of the northwest."

Like my father in 1938, had I looked out the window I would have sized up the real situation. A beautiful day—scudding clouds, a sea unnavigable with wind-blown waves. A flock of gulls, wildly circling and diving, chases a school of fish. From the looks of it, they are bluefish. The birds swoop down, the fish move further along the coast of Gardiners. The birds rise and catch the wind, chasing the fish as they parallel the coast. The clouds race, the waves race, the birds race, the fish race. They reach Bostwick Bay at the end of Gardiners in twenty minutes. When they do, another school charges over the shoal and traces the same course. It would be fun to be near the fish out there, but no boats are out in this wind.

It's just as well. I have to take a break in my fishing—I have been at it for thirty-six days. In all likelihood, since I have spent all day every day fishing and not guiding, I have cast a flyrod more than any other angler at Montauk this season. But my angling fairy tale has to take a reality detour for three days, because I committed to a job on a TV show in Washington, D.C., and there is no getting out of it. It's actually a pretty good job but it kills me to leave. The blowout on the water makes it easier to get in the car and drive to the airport.

I catch the two o'clock plane from La Guardia to Washington. Below me, the whitecaps look big, even from a great height. Nobody is fishing today. Sand running out of October's hourglass.

Part Three

WINDING UP

# October 26: Weak Coffee

THE POINT HAS BEEN relatively quiet. Blinken ran into a few blitzes at Napeague. This squares with Vic Vecchio's report of big hauls over the last week. Paul, contrary to plans, is still in town. The guy who was getting some parts for his boat didn't get them yet, or he didn't get to putting them in yet, or has been too busy pulling other boats, or maybe he went deer hunting. Whatever the reason, Paul has lost a half-dozen bookings down in North Carolina, where he should have been two days ago. He hopes to get out today.

I meet Jim Clark at Mt. Fuji. He hasn't seen a haul seine in many years and has expressed an interest in visiting with Vic and the gang. We drive through the dunes and onto the beach.

"Don't introduce me to anybody," Jim requests.

I find this puzzling, but agree.

We go over to Mitch's truck, where he is stacking nets. I ask about the deer hunting. I promised the guys that I would cook a game dinner if they bring the game.

"Saw one. No shots though."

Mitch and Wally, in fact the whole crew, share that "been-fishing-every-day" look that the guides all have by now. I probably have it too. Clothes a little funky, nobody has run a comb through their hair for a few days. For the haul seiners, add in deer hunting at 4:30 before showing up for work and you get the feeling that about this time of year, everyone knows exactly how much gas is left in their personal tank. When the season is over, the gauge will read "Empty."

Mitchell stops in the middle of his skimpy deer report. He looks at Jim.

"Hey Mr. Clark, it's Mitchell Lester. I didn't recognize you."

"Wally Bennett, Mr. Clark," his partner adds, "been a long time."

Jim looks at me. His look says, "That's why I said don't introduce me. I enjoy that moment when they put it all together and recognize me."

"You been well, Mitchell?" Jim asks. "Walter?" Jim still addresses him by the same name he used back in East Hampton Middle School.

Jim's two ex-students bring him up to date about their last twenty years or so. Mickey Miller comes over. He sports a purple turtleneck shirt visible from a quarter mile away. Then a guy I haven't seen before, wearing a smile of well-fed prosperity and a volunteer Fire Department sweatshirt—the truest emblem of localness—arrives in his pickup truck. Of course, Jim Clark knows him, too.

The new arrival, puffing on a meerschaum, delivers a short analysis of the deer season so far and then, as sometimes happens on work crews with men, the talk turns to women.

"Remember when we used to haul seine those nude beaches?" Mickey says.

Mitchell explains that the fashion crowd, which had taken over a few of the local beaches, included loads of gorgeous women. "They went topless a lot, or completely nude. I was on a surveyor's crew and we used to take our time making measurements. We'd always double check our work a few times."

"Yeah, right. Extra careful," Mickey comments with worldly sang froid.

The haul is up on the beach now. We go over to the bag. Lots of blues, lots of shad, a few dozen fluke, but just a handful of bass. When it comes time to look for a spot for the next set of the net, Jens gives it some thought. "It could be the spring tides," he says, referring to the high tide that comes with the new moon and the full moon (even if it isn't spring). "I think that's why we had such a small haul. The sand filled in over the bar."

It all looks the same to me. But Jens knows. His dad, Francis, a ninety-one-year-old veteran of haul seining, pulls up in his truck. Spunky old bird is the phrase that leaps to mind. He smiles, greets us and puffs his pipe. Francis looks at the ocean, looks at the sand and sees whatever Jens has seen. He concurs that the water looks wrong.

The crew sets off. Jim Clark and I drive the beach back toward Amagansett. He points out a guy hauling in a pound trap. "That's Calvin, also one of my students."

I have noticed Calvin before. There are about a half dozen pound traps, all with D.E.C. tags, along this stretch of beach. Their owners are among a small group allowed to net a few thousand bass during the season. There is a quota set by the state. The fishermen are given tags and every bass brought to market must be tagged.

"Calvin is a stupendous fisherman," Jim says as we drive by for a quick hello.

"Hi, Calvin, how are you?" Jim asks.

His answer—I have come to expect it by now—is completely matter-of-fact, as if running into Jim is a daily rather than a once-every-five-years experience. "Fine, Mr. Clark. How are you?"

"Good, Calvin, I'm sure you are catching fish."

We drive off.

Jim smiles. "Calvin has the knack. I remember when he was in my class, he was the first one and the last one to catch bass on a rod. Every year. Whenever the big ones charged, he always got them. I remember one year Calvin had a shop project that was languishing. 'Calvin,' I said, 'I think you should come in during exam week and work on your project.' "

Jim has a way of saying these things that is friendly, never commanding. He truly enjoys children and understands how befuddling things often seem to them, especially to teenagers.

"Monday went by, Tuesday, Wednesday, Thursday and Friday. No sign of Calvin. Finally at the end of the day on Friday he came in and asked if he could take his project home for the weekend. 'Calvin,' I said, 'I thought you were going to come in and finish your project?'

"He pulled a wad of twenties out his pocket. 'I couldn't,' he explained. 'There was a charge of bass going down the beach and this is a lot of money.' "

It was a lot of money, hundreds of dollars. Jim understood that a fishing family can't turn that down for a shop project. Anyway, Calvin, as it turned out, was simply doing fieldwork for the career Jim always knew he would go into.

We arrive back at Jim's garage. It is full of gear: the frames of kayaks in progress, a puppet stage, also in the works, for his granddaughter on Halloween (coming up fast). The workroom is spotless. The lines of a new kayak, which is fashioned from a

hi-tech Dutch plywood, are bent and angled like the clay models
that designers make for new cars. I understand how you can do
that with wet clay, but how one achieves that elegance of line
and curve with wood escapes me.

Jim cleans the bluefish that he took home from the haul seine.
"Oil and lemon in tinfoil on the grill. Don't even scale it. They'll
come off when you pull the foil away. Remember? We had that
the first day we ever fished together."

I do. "I still make it that way. I wrote about it in my column
and every so often people will tell me that they made the recipe.
Neat trick, the way the scales and skin come away and all you
have left is the fish."

≈

When I return home there is a message from Jim Levison: "Cornicelli said he heard the bass were west of the Point, down by
Gurney's. Feel like taking a ride?"

Twenty minutes later Jim pulls up. I throw my stuff in the
back. Jake, the dog, is sleeping under a pile of coats so I don't
see him as I toss my jacket on him. It doesn't matter. Jake keeps
snoring and dreaming dog dreams. Twenty minutes after that
we are at the Embassy Market in Montauk, a green-fronted grocery: Irish green, a reminder of Montauk's Irish heritage and the
Irish au pairs, cleaning ladies, plumbers, masons and gardeners
who did much of the heavy local lifting before the Latino influx
of the last dozen years.

Now Tom Desmond, the owner, has a largely Latin staff and
serves *moros y cristianos* (black beans and white rice), *pernil asado*
(roast pork), strange root vegetables that you used to see in the
Spanish markets on Columbus Avenue in Manhattan before the

upmarket franchises moved in. I spot a tray of freshly made empanadas—the Spanish version of pierogi or wontons or ravioli—crispy and filled with potatoes, chicken, beef, green peas. We order a half dozen, throw in a bottle of Melinda's Hot Sauce (a brand name that features a redhead on the label, just like my wife, Melinda).

It is warm, almost muggy, as we make our way east. The sky is rippled with clouds that look like rain in August. There is no one on the Point. No one on Turtle Cove. The albacore work tentatively in a slick by the Radar Tower. They have that calm, trouty way about them that the fish had the last day that Tom Akstens fished with me two weeks ago, but they sense our presence and are scared off by our casts. We move west to Caswell's. Dave Blinken is there, so are the bass. But, like the albacore, this blitz—you can barely call it that—is like a faded print of the vivid image of mid-October.

Levison presses west, toward Ditch Plains. Little blitzes here and there, nothing big. The bass are in, they must be hungry because bass always are, but there is no food left in the refrigerator, so to speak: The bait is leaving. We stop and watch the surfers at Ditch Plains. Only two get up for a real ride and one of them wipes out with a flourish. We sit on the bow of Jim's Parker, boots dangling over the side, eating our empanadas and hot sauce.

Jim was a homicide detective, but we never talk about it. When he does mention his former job, his tone is one you would expect from a retired mailman, not someone who dealt in dead bodies and dark souls. So I ask the question that has been on my mind but that I never get around to.

"Did it get to you, Jim? Does it still get to you?"

"You mean people without heads and bodies with their

necks slashed open so they flap like a chicken? Hey, if you do
police work, if you drive an ambulance, if you work in a hos-
pital, it all becomes part of the job. You don't even notice it.
You take a guy from under a train and two hours later you are
having dinner. I have seen the grisliest, craziest murders, the
sickest shit imaginable, but the things that get to you aren't the
serial killer crazies. With me, it's when something much less
extreme happens but it's close to your life.

"When things aren't going well in your own life, then it
really hits home. I was working the 106th Precinct, John Gotti
territory. I was in love with a woman who broke my heart and
I was depressed at the time. We had a call that there was a
suicide. We walk into a house. Nice middle-class house. The
guy was a butcher. Evidently, he sat in a chair, took a deer rifle
and put it in his mouth, which now looked like a crater of the
moon with teeth hanging out. Next to him there is a paycheck
and a bottle of booze. I pictured myself sitting in that chair. I
thought, *I don't want to look like that.* I mean it was the worst
kind of day for that guy, don't get me wrong, but in terms of
weird terrible stuff, it was minor league. Depressed guy commits
suicide. I could relate to that. Shooting, and slashing, stabbing
and stuffing people into bags—the crazy stuff—you don't see
yourself there. When normal people go off the tracks with problems like yours . . . yeah, it gets to you."

He stuffs an empanada in his mouth, dusts his hands off.
"Wind's coming around, let's get to the north side of the Point
while we still have the tide."

We run back to Montauk. It was summer when we came
out three hours ago, it is winter now. We stop in at Shagwong
for a drink. It feels toasty warm in the cheery pub after the gray
coldness. I order a bourbon old-fashioned. Jim has a beer. The

room is full of fishermen, a few of them say they have caught decent fish. A lesser few sound like they are telling the truth.

Everybody is burnt out on fishing hard. Not me, not yet. I set out to fish through October: to live the story of this month. And anyway, I *know* there are monsters still out there in the rips. We just need something to bring them to shore.

# October 27:
## Reason to Believe

≋

FOG, NO WIND. No need to start early because we cannot attempt to reach the Point in thick fog. Peter Smith Johannsen stops by around 10:00. He has long hair, and, when he's not guiding, works at this and that. In this he reminds me of myself at his age, mid-twenties, not settled, with one true star that guides his life . . . fishing. He drives an International Harvester whose top lifts up in heavy winds. While driving, this requires him to reach between the seats to retrieve a screwdriver and tighten a loose screw where the top is pulling away from the windshield.

"Strange, but girls love this car," he tells me. The truth of the matter is girls probably love Peter and they take the car as part of the package.

All across the Napeague flats, the fog shrouds everything, but when we reach the Crabby Cowboy it is considerably clearer. We drive down to Gin Beach. To the east, whatever mix the weather and tidal cauldron of Montauk has served up today no longer includes fog.

We get in the boat and blast, wasting no time prospecting the north side. No bass, no slicks, no Black Holes. The albies are making the same shy showing that they did yesterday. I have had my fill of albies, especially uncooperative ones. If there is a tribe of bass somewhere near, still within the aura of the Point, that is the only thing I want to find.

Peter agrees. We speed past the Point, slide around the turn to the south side and open her wide. If Cornicelli was right about the blitz two days ago; if what we saw yesterday was the tail end of something that had happened earlier in the day; and if the bass are indeed moving west, then we need to be somewhere between Ditch Plains and Napeague.

Just west of Ditch Plains, where the cliffs end and the strand at Montauk Village starts, there is a wide bay. It is calm today except for an inviting patch of dark, nervous water. The only other person in sight is a lone kayaker with a spinning rod. He moves toward the nervous water. When a motor powered craft moves toward a hint of something, that doesn't mean much; however, when a kayaker makes a move, it is a more considered one.

Peter notices a slick of fish oil, like yellow detergent. The fish are here somewhere and so is the bait. The water darkens. The bass break through. The Black Hole is almost as intense as I have seen it all month, but slightly different. Two weeks ago you could drive your boat right into the feeding mass and they would take no notice of you. Today they are skittish and the blitz is short-lived: up for two minutes, or one minute, or twenty seconds, then they go down, then they come up again a hundred yards away. My guess is there is bait, maybe not much of it, but it is all there is so the fish are prowling the bay, rounding up stragglers.

It requires finesse to get within casting range of these bass: good casting, too. Peter handles the boat part of the equation well. When the bass surface, he guns the engine and then, when we are on line with the fish, he shuts down and we glide into the pack. I must cast before they sense us, but my casting is not together. Maybe it's the three day lay-off or maybe it's trying to assimilate all of the advice that Caucci, Paul, Blinken, Amanda, Sedotti and Levison have offered

Cooch: *Drift more.* Paul: *Don't turn your body until you release the backcast.* Amanda: *No slack.* Sedotti: *Come over the top.* Blinken: *Throw.* Levison: *Don't throw.*

There are a lot of voices in my head.

*Slow down. Slow down. Slow down.* If I do that, I will cast well, or at least good enough. I'm like a pitcher whose fastball isn't working and who must turn to his curve; slowing down will fix 90 percent of the problems in my saltwater cast.

I hook up, bring my fish in and release him. The Black Hole materializes again a hundred yards east. Materializes is an accurate way to describe it, much the way that people come and go as they are teleported around the universe in space operas—first a shimmering, then a physical presence.

Peter chases the pack. "Your turn," I tell him. In short order he catches a fish. We pass some hours that way: chasing, easing in, catching. From time to time the Black Hole is gone for ten or fifteen minutes. It moves back and forth over a mile-long path. On one of the longer intermissions in the striper show, Peter opens a container of black and green olives tossed with rosemary and red pepper flakes, also some sheep's milk cheese. Peter falls on the quiet side of the guiding scale. He stays calm, talks quietly, doesn't press the angler or the fish too hard.

We are still alone except for the kayaker. Good thing, any other engine noise and those bass would be gone. Now, the birds start to come in. They see the dark water before we do.

They hover, screeing and flapping. Their massed body English accentuates the movements of the school of bass. The birds hold, they reposition slightly, the fish come up, the water froths. The sound of the cheering stadium crowd that the fish made before the full moon has come down a few decibels. Now they call to mind a smallish concert hall ringing with applause.

Watching, chasing, catching—our plate is full. As the afternoon wears on, the sky darkens and the wind grows cold. After twenty—maybe it was thirty, or even fifty—surface blitzes, we have caught our fill. It is a long ride back. Just off Caswell's, we spot Wally's boat, the *Mischief,* very near the rocks at the western end of the cove. Blinken is there too, also Scott Holder in his brand new black boat, a gorgeous fishing machine.

We follow Wally into a small blitz. Ernie, who is also on board for a busman's holiday, fights a fish and shouts at us over his shoulder, "Where the hell were you guys all day? There were albies at the Point!"

Peter deadpans, "Yeah, I heard they catch them sometimes right by the lighthouse."

Following boats, avoiding rocks and trying to horn in on the small blitz—there isn't much percentage in this. We have had a whole day, a whole bay, a whole blitz all to ourselves. We run back to the harbor. The moon tide is so strong that it has exposed sandbars inside the harbor that I haven't seen all season. On this tide, if there were fish by the lighthouse, they would be going bananas in the raging rip. But all the fish we found were further west. The blitzing schools appear to have left the Point. Or, if they haven't fully left, they are about to.

# October 28: Finis Terre

≋

A PERFECT FALL DAY, except if you want to fish. High fleecy
clouds, like scampering lambs, pushed across the October sky by
winds up to 40 miles per hour. It's Saturday: Melinda and Lily
are with me. Lucy will take the train out after her volleyball
match. The blowout on the water allows me to spend family
time with undivided loyalties.

My brother, Bob, is in from California. We squeeze into
the Jeep: Melinda, Lily, Bobby and me. We cut straight across
Amagansett to the ocean. The west wind hammers the incoming tide. We park the car and walk the beach. There is a line
of mussel shells at the high-water mark. When we have
walked a half mile, I notice that the tide is coming up fast. I
turn and look at the car.

*Damn!* I should have remembered how extreme the tides
have been for the last few days. Looking back against the glare
I can't tell if the incoming water has reached my car or not. I
take off as fast as I can. Running—not jogging—a half mile on
sand is tough. I have visions of a surge picking up my car. Worse,
the car isn't even mine, I borrowed it.

Shortly before my lungs and my legs give out I see that what

I thought was water lapping against the car is just the sun glinting off the sand, a mini-mirage. Whew!

Bobby suggests a drive by Westlake Marina at Montauk. Years ago, he would fish out here with Art Munday for tuna and sharks. We pull up to West Lake Lodge, the bar they drank at. There is a middle-of-the-afternoon crowd—i.e., not many people and, for health reasons, those that are there probably shouldn't be. The gal behind the bar wears big hoop earrings and has a whiskey and cigarette laugh. She has the air of a person who has had a particularly rough day. I have the feeling this might be a permanent condition. In order to be heard, I have to talk over the college football but finally I succeed in ordering an old-fashioned. Bobby has a scotch. Melinda has a beer, and Lily gets a Sprite with cherries.

"I used to know a guy who fished out of here. Art Munday," Bobby says. "Do you know if he is still around?"

"No," she says, curtly.

I had forgotten about Art until Bobby mentioned him today. Art rode shotgun for Dutch Schultz during Prohibition. He was also a labor organizer. When Franco staged his coup in Spain in 1936, Art joined the Abraham Lincoln Brigade to fight fascists. After the West abandoned the Loyalists and Stalin did, too, a disgusted Munday came back to the States and holed up in Montauk. There are a lot of people who ended up here because there is no next place to go after you hit Montauk.

Art lived in a little apartment behind the bar. To pay his bills he became a charter captain for tuna. "When you hunt for tuna," Bobby says, "there are always sharks swimming around, so Art became a shark hunter, too. He had a .45 on board (many shark captains do the same in order to deliver the coup de grace to their dangerous quarry). He brought it back from Spain. He liked .45s, said they were designed for use by cavalry officers with the idea that that would pack enough power to drop a horse at fifty yards.

"One day we had spent a few hours setting up a chum slick. Another boat came bearing down on our slick. To keep them from churning it up and ruining our morning's work, he fired the .45 across their bow"—Bob pauses—"well, almost across their bow. He claimed that if they had continued on their course then he would have continued firing. For all I know, he might have."

The cold wind finds its way through the windows of the bar. We drink up and leave. A small commercial fishing boat has just moored. Their going out on a day like this brings home the difference between sportfishing and fishing as the only way you have to put bread on the table. Bobby approaches the boat. "I was just wondering. I used to have a friend here, Art Munday. Is he still around?"

The fisherman, his face red with windburn, keeps heaving equipment as he answers. "Art Munday, yeah, used to live out back. He's still alive, I hear, in a home somewhere."

On the way back to Gerard Drive we stop at the seafood store in Amagansett. I have a hunger for bay scallops, tiny and sweet, fresh out of Gardiners Bay. Sean, behind the counter, says, "Too expensive, we don't carry them, but if you want some, make a right on Abrahams Path and just by the railroad tracks you'll see a sign for fresh scallops."

We follow his directions, make a left down a long driveway and stop in front of a low, white shack. Bob and I go in and order two pounds of scallops. The proprietor of the shop is none other than Calvin, Jim Clark's former student. It stands to reason if anybody is going to have in-demand seafood it would be the best fisherman out here.

My friend, cookbook author Sheila Lukins, is coming to dinner along with Amanda, Blinken and Josh. When she arrives, she puts on her apron and joins me at the stove. We pan-roast red peppers and onions, puree them and pass them through a sieve. Then we dust the scallops with turmeric and green peppercorns before roasting them off in hot oil. Bobby is a good grillman (and will tell you so). I dispatch him into the howling gale in the backyard to barbecue the shell steaks, which will be served with defrosted cherry sauce from the big dinner with Paul a few weeks back. Lucy shows up in a cab from the train station and jumps in on prep detail.

After dinner we put on a video, *One Touch of Venus,* starring Ava Gardner. It is a wonderful S. J. Perelman adaptation of a stage play, with music by Kurt Weill, the kind of thing that Lucy, in particular, adores. It is the story of an employee at a department store who captures the heart of Venus, Goddess of Love (father Zeus has sent her down to earth to experience earthly love among mortals). It is coy, funny, satirical, and Ava Gardner is beautiful enough that I think if there is a real Venus, she probably looks like this.

Midway through the movie, the self-adoring owner of the department store, Whitfield Savory II, is smitten by Venus, but she has absolutely no interest in him. In order to impress her, the unsavory Mr. Savory tells her in a seductive tone (like the one he might use to close a lingerie purchase), "I have arranged everything. Lunch at the Mum and Quiet Club then off to Montauk Point for a candlelight dinner at the Sand and Surf Yacht Club!"

It makes us all feel rather swanky to hear our dear unelegant Montauk held up as a sophisticated destination whose mere mention might secure the conquest of the Goddess of Love.

# October 29:
# An Early Squall

≈

"UNTIL THEY THINK warm days will never cease," John Keats wrote in his ode "To Autumn," a poem that I have thought of many times these past weeks. When snow comes on the twenty-ninth of October, as it has begun to do this morning, it is safe to say those warm days have ceased.

Lucy and I drive down to the beach in my Jeep. Shafts of sun break through the cloud cover. They light up a line of snow squalls. The snow, driven by a biting west wind, covers our windshield. For the very first time since I came to the East End, I don't even think about trying to fish. In fact I don't even think about getting out of the car. Cold!

The geese fly low, the gulls sit and appear to shiver, but the ocean doesn't look so bad. The wild seas of the last few days have flattened out some in the wind. Come to think of it, although today may be a bust, tomorrow . . . well fishing always has a lot of tomorrow in it.

# October 30: Cold Hands

≋

I CALL AMANDA AT 5:30 A.M. The wind is still strong out of the west, but Vic plans to haul and Amanda has told me she wants to see it done. I let her phone ring a half dozen times. She doesn't answer.

Amanda has taken a job with a landscaping firm. This will allow her to divide her time between landscaping and guiding. She wants to get her certification as a landscape architect so that she has a real business, instead of counting on guiding to carry her through life. "This way," she explained, "I can afford to guide. Big difference, now I *have* to guide."

I call again and let it ring until she picks up. "See you in fifteen minutes," she says in a groggy voice. She arrives, true to her word, and we head to the beach. It's early but Calvin is already out pulling nets. Up ahead, I see Vic's convoy coming through the dunes. Jens and Mitchell, pretty much running on auto pilot at this stage of the project, lay out the net from their dory. On shore the guys still talk about deer (which they have yet to shoot). Then the conversation turns to football games and naps and how delicious they are on a Sunday afternoon, how you fade in and out of the game while children run around the house, but it still doesn't keep you from sleeping.

Once the dory has finished its circuit, we discover the clutch has gone out on one of the winches: Next comes the sound of cold tools on cold broken metal, lots of banging and prying as the guys try to repair the clutch. Finally, the universal fix-it, a roll of duct tape, holds the mechanism together long enough to pull up the nets. The haul is not spectacular: a bunch of flounder, a few shad, a fair number of mullet and menhaden and forty or fifty bass, the largest about twenty-four inches.

When it comes time to release the bass, Vic demonstrates for a new assistant. "Always hold the big ones next to your body; they have less chance of wriggling free before you get them into the water," he explains.

Amanda doesn't know much about haul seines but she is an expert at reviving and releasing bass. She sees the scientists heaving them into the surf. She is used to a more gentle release, which is what is required after fighting a fish to exhaustion on rod and reel, but not so necessary when they are still frisky after being netted. She walks her bass down to the water's edge. Without waders, in fact just in jeans and a sweater, she catches a wave that soaks her. "Go back sweetie," she says as she sends a striper back to its home.

When the work is done, the cold gets to her. "No problem, I'm just cold. I'll get warm," she says but that means she's done driving the beaches for now. I drop her off at her Volvo at Mt. Fuji and stop in at Harvey Bennett's for an appointed rendezvous with Peter Smith Johannsen. Like me, he doesn't want to give up on the year yet. We don't have a prayer of getting out in a boat—the wind on the northside has scratched that from today's playbook—so we drive until we see some sitting gulls. Earlier in the season we would have ignored them. Now, with slimmer pickings so late in the run, we look for any sign of hope. We reason that with a whole beach to hang out on, maybe the gulls have chosen this place to sit because there is bait nearby. Our attitude toward the gulls is somewhat like that of a man with a receding hairline looking for signs of new hair growth. Lots of hope, little cause for it.

Peter sees a slick and asks, "Are you ambitious?"

This means do I want to get out of the warm car, rig up my rod, put on my waders and stand in the cold wind casting?

"I don't know, are you?"

"Well, what do you think?"

And so on, back and forth, a kind of *I'll do it if you do* game of chicken. There will be plenty of time for not fishing in the coming months, we figure, and a sign of life, such as a slick, is reason for some hope.

I wader up and Peter puts on hip boots. I slip into the cold water. The beach drops off into a trough, so once I reach water to my waist I stop. Otherwise, any swell will go over the top of my waders. Peter, on the other hand, knows exactly where to wade to the sandbar that lies on the other side of the trough. He casts. I cast. Half a dozen casts and my hands are too cold. I retreat while Peter gives it a few more tries.

I notice a house going up right next to the parking lot. At current prices, that means someone is spending millions of dollars to have a view of asphalt and cars. When I think of this house, when I think of the seven houses in the virgin dunes that have inexplicably passed muster with the town board at Napeague, I long for a tidal wave, an act of God to purify the shore. I don't consider the people who own the houses and the heartache this will mean. I surely don't wish them harm. I simply want the pride homes, as I have come to think of them, gone. But if wishes were realities, I would be knee deep in bass.

# October 31: Paraclete

≋

OCTOBER IS IMPATIENT to be done. A northwest gale, 35 knots, delivers a message from the tundra: *"Here comes winter."* On the south shore, though, the wind keeps the surf down so that Vic can set his nets. Jim Levison joins me to take some photos of the haul seine. We watch the guys bring in one haul, just a few bass. It is clear by now that *The Event,* The Run that started with the rainbait moving out of Accabonac Neck six weeks ago, is ending, not with a shout but a whisper. Sometime, maybe three weeks from now, the herring may show. We see a few gannets diving, a sign that although the season is moving along, perhaps they are a harbinger of one last hurrah.

Vic doesn't think so, but he is not laying any bets one way or the other. Peter Smith Johannsen arrives and, as he does, we see a few bass busting on the surface. We look more intently. To our right, diving birds and white water under them signal a blitz. We drive to it. Too far out for fly rods. Too far out, in fact, for the spinfishermen who have been drawn to the same school. The fish are moving fast to the west. We drive. Every time the school feints toward the shore we wait. Two or three times we get out of the car, rods at the ready, but the bass never come close enough for a shot.

We chase the blitz for two hours. As long as they continue to tease us we are game to follow. Peter's radiator hose busts. We tape it up. Peter has a slicker but no boots. I have waders and gloves but no slicker. Jim has no gloves. Taken in sum we comprise one reasonably equipped angler.

Peter notices something. "Look there, caterpillar tracks heading west."

Hot dog! They have opened a cut to Georgica Pond! All the bait that has been trapped in the salt pond will rush out and every bass within twenty miles will line up to feast on the outflow.

We follow the tracks. Where are the birds? The bass? The fishermen?

We see a steam shovel in front of us. There is no cut at Georgica. What's happened is that a work crew has brought some earthmoving equipment across the beach. They are lifting railroad ties, and digging a trench to reinforce the dunes that abut a recently completed home. One good nor'easter on a spring tide and that retaining wall will be an offshore reef. Oh well, a good day's pay for the workmen, a good whack for the contractor and I suppose the seigneur in the big house feels, at least momentarily, that Nature takes orders from him.

Moving toward Wainscott to exit the beach, we come upon a scene that could well have been lifted from a Buñuel movie: though it is thirty-five degrees or so (in the teens if you consider wind-chill), a beautiful woman stands on the beach in a bare-shouldered bridal dress. The brisk wind catches her veil and ruffles it like a pennant. She carries a bouquet and twirls around with a look of great joy. She is neither a figment of a cinematographer's dream nor a lunatic. It is a fashion shoot. A warmly dressed photographer with a whirlwind of an assistant flits here and there snapping photos while the frozen faux bride does her best to give the impression that she is outdoors on a warm summer day, having the time of her life.

For no other reason than we are out and have nowhere to go and it is the last day of October, Peter and Jim take up my suggestion that we have a look at the Point. Off Turtle Cove we see a dragger fighting the waves to make it to port.

On the north bar, the wind drives the incoming seas onshore. The air is cold as January. Still, even in this, there are three fishermen standing in the water. If there are fish around, then the wind and the sea will drive bait into this shore. One of these hard-core surfcasters makes it out to a rock about thirty feet offshore. He half crouches, half stands to maintain his balance as he snaps off a cast. Because faith, or perhaps courage, is sometimes rewarded, a bass hits his lure. For us to be able to see the strike in this roiling sea, it has to be a furious hit. The gulls that inhabit the rocky spit notice the action. Three of them take wing.

Once in the air they need only to spread their wings and the incoming gale keeps each of them aloft like the white dove in Piero della Francesca's soothingly mystical "The Baptism of Christ," in which the outstretched wings of the Holy Spirit frame a seashell from which John the Baptist pours a stream of water.

In front of us, the sea is green and frenzied. The sky hangs heavy and gray. The rod bends. The angler stands straight and pulls back. A wide shaft of sunlight streams down on Block Island in the distance: In contrast with the dreary sky and sea all around, the island gleams as if it had cliffs of gold.

# A Month Later

≋

OCTOBER'S WARM SPELL became the coldest November anyone remembers. I divide my time between the East End and "civilian life" in the city. Driving back and forth on the Long Island Expressway is a most effective shock therapy in leading me back to the world of newspapers, bills, dental appointments, gasbag political pundits, humbling homework problems with the kids, a busted lever on my office chair and the interminable repairs that have turned the street in front of my house into a fair replication of the trenchworks at the Battle of the Somne.

I am gone from the East End, but still a short car ride away. All through November I keep coming back. To be sure, The Run has ended, but, with luck, the herring will come and with them the huge cow stripers who have waited in the bottoms of the rips for this last great feast before they move to their winter berths.

The guides are all gone except for Wally Johnsen and Jim Levison. Harvey Bennett spends more time hunting ducks and geese than he does fishing. The water-fowling is good, as it tends to be when the weather sucks.

Just after Thanksgiving, Harvey calls: "Don't know if you

are still fishing, but the gannets are on herring at Gin Beach, diving in such shallow water I am surprised they are not breaking their necks in the sand."

Shortly after that, Paul calls as well. He has just returned from Harkers Island and is as anxious as I am to learn if the herring run materialized and, with it, the big bass. "Wally said there were whales and porpoises crashing herring right outside the entrance to the harbor!" he reports.

I don't even bother stopping by my house, I go straight from Brooklyn to meet Paul at Napeague. Offshore there are diving gannets and below them rafts of sea ducks. When the ducks take wing, the disturbance they make on the water looks deceptively like a bass blitz. There must be at least ten thousand ducks, in large groups, off the white sand beaches. As we reach Hither Hills a large mastiff devours the guts of a seal that has washed up in the surf.

We drive to the Point, on the north side. A cold, clear day, temperature in the twenties, wind out of the west, and gannets— thousands of them—on the rip right in front of the lighthouse. They are solidly packed, yet fluid. The big birds drop in free fall, hit the water like cannonballs, rise up and take their position at the top of the formation for another descent. It is a cascade of white feathers. If I squint a little, it looks very much like a waterfall seen from the side, a frothy cataract extending out from the cliffs, very like Niagara.

We look hard at the splashes. No bass. If there are that many birds presumably on that many herring and no bass, The Run is done for this year.

As I write this in midwinter, watching the snow fall in Brooklyn, I think of the last scene in *Walkabout*, a film by Ni- colas Roeg. In that movie, a teenage girl and her brother are stranded in the Australian outback. They are befriended by an aborigine boy on his vision quest, or "walkabout" as it is known in his religion. A beautiful girl on the cusp of womanhood, the boy, likewise, about to become a man, the tension between them, the fight to survive.

At the end of the movie, the girl has grown up and married some average guy. She smokes a cigarette, listens to something mindless on the radio, pours herself a drink, prepares a dinner from shrink-wrapped supermarket adequacies. As she fixes the meal, her mind drifts back to a scene in the wild with her brother and the young bushman. They stand under a waterfall. The sun beats down and the water washes over them.

In the same way, I see Montauk before me. My Indian summer was a walkabout into something perfect and outside of time. Thinking back to any moment of that month brings up images rich with detail and power. It was not Eden. I didn't eat a forbidden apple. Nobody expelled me, but my October pulls me like that ancient garden. And though neither you, nor I, nor anyone, can return to Eden, we can all make it back to Montauk when the butterflies and the bass stream south again.